T0113371

Solidarity in the Conversation of Humankind

Solidarity in the Conversation of Humankind

The Ungroundable Liberalism of Richard Rorty

NORMAN GERAS

VERSO

London • New York

First published by Verso 1995
© Norman Geras 1995
All rights reserved

Verso
UK: 6 Meard Street, London W1V 3HR
USA: 29 West 35th Street, New York, NY 10001–2291

Verso is the imprint of New Left Books

ISBN: 978-0-86091-659-8

British Library Cataloguing in Publication Data
A catalogue record for this book is available from the
British Library

Library of Congress Cataloging-in-Publication Data
Geras, Norman, 1943–
    Solidarity in the conversation of humankind : the ungroundable
liberalism of Richard Rorty / Norman Geras
        p. cm.
    Includes bibliographical references and index.
    ISBN: 978-0-86091-659-8
    1. Rorty, Richard. 2. Man. 3. Solidarity. 4. Liberalism.
5. World War, 1939–1945—Jews—Rescue. I. Title.
B945.R524G47 1995
191—dc20   95–1097
                                                        CIP

Typeset by M Rules
Printed in Great Britain by Biddles Ltd, Guildford and Kings Lynn

To my sisters and my brother

Contents

Introduction

This book aims at continuing a conversation. It takes for interlocutor a writer who is himself today indefatigable in engaging with the ideas of others, Richard Rorty.

Rorty reads and he reads. He interprets and reinterprets, contextualizes, reflects, proposes, all under the sign of conversation as a compelling virtue. His work ranges widely over issues and authors, over thinkers past and contemporary, philosophers, novelists, literary critics. The focus of this book, on the other hand, is narrower. Though its principal themes of conversation may be situated by reference to a number of different framing contexts, they form nevertheless, the themes, a small, closely related group.

One relevant framing context is this. Just over ten years ago I published a book about Marx which attempted to lay to rest the claim that he had dispensed with the idea of a general human nature. The view that he had done so was then popular amongst Marxists, especially those of structuralist inclination, the many who had been influenced by the work of Louis Althusser. More broadly, a common notion in the culture of the left at the time, in the arguments of socialists, feminists and others of progressive or radical outlook, was that the concept of an intrinsic human nature was to be rejected. My *Marx and Human Nature* sought both to show that the claim about Marx was wrong and to rebut this common tendency within left argument.

There is less interest today in the Marxological aspect of

1

the question. The anti-humanist reading of Marx is not so propagated or so popular, and Marx is being less obsessively read now anyway. But opinions and advocacy dismissive of any intrinsic or universal human nature persist. They are sustained by other developments in the intellectual culture, in particular by post-structuralist and post-modernist currents of thought. Many of the same people who formerly took their distance from the concept of human nature as Marxists, now dismiss it as 'post'-ists of one kind and another. Not that this makes much difference to the shape or substance of the issues at stake. Indeed, it is precisely a sense that the denial of any human nature has been made no more persuasive by these changed bases of intellectual support for it that impels me here. There seems to be a point in continuing the conversation.

That context is mine, however, it is not Richard Rorty's. He has had no public relationship to the argument about Marx and human nature. Here, then, is a recontextualization. Another relevant backdrop to the preoccupations of the present book is anti-foundationalism. There are different aspects to this. One of them is philosophical pragmatism and anti-realism, an overt impatience on Rorty's part with any idea of things just as they are in themselves – that is, apart from language, apart from all description, apart from the uses to which people might want to put them. This is a main concern and repeated emphasis through all his writing, registered and pursued in connection with a variety of problems and a whole array of different thinkers. By its very generality, however, it touches also on the particularity which is of interest to me, human nature. It does so because another side of it is what is called 'anti-essentialism'. Integral to the general anti-foundationalist theme is Rorty's insistence that nothing can have an intrinsic nature; the latter notion is, according to him, no more than a remnant of the idea of God.

The general anti-foundationalist theme yields, therefore, the more specific trope: absence of any intrinsic human nature. Not Rorty's most central or pressing concern perhaps, the issue of human nature is, all the same, recurrent within his discourse. Responding to him, I make it more central in my own. I do not on that account ignore the general anti-foundationalist and anti-realist philosophical standpoint to which it belongs. One chapter here is devoted to considering precisely that. But it is moved away from the centre of the discussion. Thus, I converse with Rorty on topics which are his, but I change their relative weights and places in the conversation. Why, however, address these topics in dialogue especially with Rorty? An apt answer might be: just contingently so. Still, there is a bit more that can be said. First, and as already suggested, I take Rorty's work as embodying certain typically post-modern commitments and arguments, ones which I believe need to be critically opposed. Rorty himself, it is only fair to note in this regard, despite having made play for a time with the post-modernist label, now regrets having done so. But I do not take his work as any kind of model of the broad, and loose, intellectual trend that goes under this label. I merely examine some of the views which, whatever his attitude to the label, he does undoubtedly share with its more unqualified enthusiasts.

Second, Rorty is in any case a powerful and a congenial interlocutor, which may be reason enough. With enormous learning and an impressive command of different philosophical traditions, analytic and continental, he writes lucidly, without pretension, and with force and humour. He is generally tolerant and inclusive in his modes of address. He puts to the test the convictions of anyone attached to the ideas he urges us now to leave behind. Speaking for myself, if I have not been persuaded, I have certainly sometimes been worried by him on some of the matters to be treated in these pages, have been made to think and think again.

Third and above all, though, it is the values Rorty espouses that engage me and which have encouraged this effort of response. That may surprise some people, since he describes himself as a liberal or, on occasion, a social democrat, whereas I have been my adult life, and remain, some kind of Marxist.

3

But I mean here Rorty's values, and not his overall political outlook. If we place in parenthesis some likely differences about the relative virtues and faults of capitalism as a social and economic system, Rorty's values, the values of a radical liberalism, are somewhere close to mine, the values at the heart of the socialist project. It is because they are that I am challenged to probe whether, for example, freedom, justice, the hope of minimizing avoidable suffering, could be well served by anti-foundationalist commitments.

This evokes willy-nilly a third framing context for the conversation. The latter takes place against a political background today of some fiercely intolerant particularisms, religious, national, resurgently racist; of hatreds and cruelties such as have been focused lately for the whole world by the so-called 'ethnic cleansing' in former Yugoslavia and the wave of bloodshed in Rwanda. These things, of course, are not caused by debates amongst academics, philosophers or cultural critics. Nevertheless, one may be allowed to wonder how setting aside the universalist claim of a common human nature, as Rorty with currently so many others from this rather detached milieu would have us do, could conceivably help. Can this really be a vital task now from within any liberal, democratic, socialist, or other such progressive outlook? Rorty is himself aware on some level of the question, for he gives attention to the likely sources of interpersonal solidarity and of its absence, to the relation or the non-relation between it and universalist notions of humanity. He invites us to think about this in connection with perhaps the most staining enormity of our century as far as murderous hatreds go, the Nazi genocide against the Jews. I address myself to his arguments on this matter.

The pages that follow, then, are in one perspective a kind of sequel and companion to my earlier *Marx and Human Nature*; they take up again its principal concern. In a second perspective, resuming this by way of a consideration of Richard Rorty's work, they proffer critical discussion of ideas much canvassed today by the sponsors of post-modernity. They attempt finally, in a third perspective and following

Rorty himself, to assess these currently fashionable ideas in relation both to the values of a progressive politics and to their extreme and violent denial. The basic organization of the book is this. In Chapter 1 I consider a hypothesis of Rorty's about solidarity. I examine the speculation he offers about the motives of those who came to the rescue of Jews in Nazi Europe, and I show that it is not borne out by existing research or by the testimony of rescuers themselves. In Chapter 2 I explore, as one likely source of Rorty's speculation, his various usages with respect to a 'human nature', and I point out the serious tensions and inconsistencies between them. In Chapter 3 I defend universalist modes of moral thinking, of the sort evident in the testimony of rescuers, by trying to show why Rorty's proposed alternative – a solidarity, and a liberalism, without foundations – is neither persuasive nor conducive to democratic ways of thought. Chapter 4 concludes the volume with an engagement with Rorty's anti-realism. I argue: that there is a formal, vitiating parallel between his positions on this matter and his positions on human nature; and, adverting once more to the Holocaust, that his 'ironist' attitude to questions of truth would, unflinchingly held, leave one intellectually defenceless in the face of injustice and oppression.

This book was conceived and written as a single, developing argument: its several themes to connect up into a relatively unified whole. I have tried also in the composition of it, however, to ensure that each chapter will have, despite a limited number of references back and forward, a certain self-contained, free-standing character; enabling any reader interested most particularly, say, in the issue of rescue, or in arguments about human nature – and so on – to consult the relevant chapter and leave it at that. How far I have been successful, either in the unifying or in the self-containing enterprise, is not of course for me to say.

I have benefited from the opportunity to present and get reactions to some part of what I have to say here at seminars both in my own Department and at other Universities. I am grateful for the many helpful comments that I had on these occasions. More generally, I should like to record my gratitude to the Department of Government at the University of Manchester, of which I have been a member now for more than a quarter of a century, and in which I have been able to pursue the interests I wanted to pursue and to do the work I wanted to do, in the company of good friends and colleagues. For specific discussion of Rorty's ideas at various times during the last two or three years, I thank Shane O'Neill, Mark Harvey and Roy Bhaskar, each of whom generously, and also enjoyably, helped me in the process of clarifying my own ideas; without incurring any responsibility, naturally, for anything I think and say.

The love and support I get from my wife and daughters, Adèle, Sophie and Jenny, I have depended on and drawn strength from yet once more. All of them know directly for themselves the pains and the pleasures of writing – though *for* themselves, perhaps, more the pleasures of it, and in me, more the pains. One of the pleasures, in any event, is to be just at the point I am now, and it is thanks above all to the three of them that I am.

Manchester, November 1994

Richard Rorty and the Righteous Among the Nations

In the early hours of 2 February 1945, several hundred Russian prisoners escaped from Mauthausen. Apart from the killing centres in Poland, Mauthausen, not far from Linz in Upper Austria, was the most brutal of camps in the Nazi concentrationary system, those forced to labour in its stone quarry having a life expectancy of one to three months. The escapees were from the remnant (by then a mere 570) of some 4700 Soviet officers sent to Mauthausen less than a year before, who were being subjected to a regime even harsher than the norm there and aimed specifically at destroying them all. They were dying at a rate of between twenty and thirty every day. Some of these men, once they had got beyond the outer wall, were too weak to go further, and more than half of them were caught and summarily killed during the same day. In the end only a dozen are known to have made good their escape and survived.

In anticipation of the advance of the Red Army, these Russian prisoners had placed their hopes in finding succour among the civilian population, but in vain. Their recapture was widely witnessed, in fright and sympathetic horror or with ghoulish curiosity, and the SS and local Nazi party encouraged citizen participation in the manhunt. It was forthcoming: the fugitives, many of them begging for their lives, were simply slaughtered.

In general, residents of the area who were approached by the fleeing men to shelter them, declined under public threat of lethal reprisals. Maria and Johann Langthaler, however – with four of their children living with them – did not. Taking in one man who came to their door, Maria persuaded her husband, at first alarmed at the awful risk, that they should harbour him. They then also took in a second man. Both of these hid there at the Langthalers for three months until the end of the war. We have Maria Langthaler's explanation of why she acted as she did. She was obligated as a Christian, she said, to help when someone was in need: 'The Lord God is for the whole world, not only for the Germans. It is a community and there one must help. I did not ask them to which party they belong, I asked nothing at all; that made no difference to me. Only because they were human beings.'[1]

Only because they were human beings. Although the men she took into her home were in fact Russian prisoners of war, I let this story symbolize a continent-wide phenomenon of that era: against a background of the persecution and massacre of the Jews of Europe, in which very many Europeans were complicit as participants whilst very many more stood by in fearful or indifferent passivity, some – not nearly as many, but still, more than just a handful – were yet willing to take risks, often terrible risks, in their efforts to harbour and rescue those in danger. I want to address here the question of how common amongst these rescuers was the sort of reason voiced by Maria Langthaler.

I

I start from the contrary hypothesis: that it was not very common. This is the view of Richard Rorty, which I shall report first at some length. Rorty begins his essay, 'Solidarity', as follows:

> If you were a Jew in the period when the trains were running to Auschwitz, your chances of being hidden by your gentile neighbours were greater if you lived in Denmark or Italy than if you lived in Belgium. A common way of describing this difference is

by saying that many Danes and Italians showed a sense of human solidarity which many Belgians lacked.

Asserting that the basic explanatory notion in this connection is that of being 'one of us', Rorty goes on to argue that this notion carries less force when its sense is 'one of us human beings' than it does when referring to some narrower grouping, such as 'a comrade in the movement' or a 'fellow Catholic'. Typically, he claims, 'it contrasts with a "they" which is also made up of human beings – the wrong sort of human beings.'

> Consider . . . those Danes and those Italians. Did they say, about their Jewish neighbours, that they deserved to be saved because they were fellow human beings? Perhaps sometimes they did, but surely they would usually, if queried, have used more parochial terms to explain why they were taking risks to protect a given Jew – for example, that this particular Jew was a fellow Milanese, or a fellow Jutlander, or a fellow member of the same union or profession, or a fellow bocce player, or a fellow parent of small children . . . [Or] Consider . . . the attitude of contemporary American liberals to the unending hopelessness and misery of the young blacks in American cities. Do we say that these people must be helped because they are our fellow human beings? We may, but it is much more persuasive, morally as well as politically, to describe them as our fellow *Americans* – to insist that it is outrageous that an *American* should live without hope.

Our sense of solidarity, Rorty then says again, is strongest with collectivities 'smaller and more local than the human race' and 'imaginative identification' easier; whereas '"because she is a human being" is a weak, unconvincing explanation of a generous action.'[2]

Some general philosophical issues raised by Rorty's argument are dealt with in Chapters 2 and 3 of this book. My concern here is only with the hypothesis about the rescuers' explanations of their actions.[3] I shall take it as he presents it. I shall focus, that is to say, on the question of their motives.

But I need to guard, then, against one possible misunderstanding, as I now briefly do.

Let us extend Rorty's comparison to cover the Netherlands. Where only 56 per cent of the Jews in Belgium survived the 'Final Solution', as compared with 99 per cent and 83 per cent, respectively, of the Jews of Denmark and Italy, the greatest catastrophe outside eastern Europe was actually that visited on the Dutch Jews. More than 70 per cent of them perished. This comparison now secretes a fact of some apparent relevance to the question to be pursued. No more than 10 per cent of the Jews living in Belgium at the start of the war were Belgian citizens. The rest were recent immigrants or refugees. In the Netherlands, on the other hand, these proportions were almost exactly reversed, only 10 per cent of the Jews there being refugees. A considerably smaller proportion of the Dutch than of the Belgian Jews was saved, in other words, notwithstanding any advantage the former might be thought to have had on account of longer established citizenship and social integration.

This fact however, though certainly relevant to Rorty's reflections, is not by itself decisive – and not only because of some further hypothesis we might venture as to modes of 'imaginative identification' by Belgians which reached across the divide of citizenship. The point is that such comparisons simplify a very complex historical issue. Identification with and effective aid and support to the Jews on the part of any given national population in Europe was only one of the factors governing their fate. Some others were the type and degree, if any, of German political and administrative control in each country; the time at which the Nazis moved decisively to deport its Jews to the death sites and the military prospect then – how soon a German defeat in the war might be anticipated; the response also of the Jews themselves in each country; the accessibility or otherwise of a secure haven (as the Danes had in nearby Sweden); and still other things beside. There is by now a large analytical literature on all this.[4] To focus on the reasons of individual rescuers is to abstract only one feature from a much larger picture. With that clarification made, I shall myself adopt the same focus nonetheless. If the rescuers' solidarity and their motives for it constituted only one factor in the outcome, they were an important factor. And there are reasons I shall come to presently for caring about what their motives were.

The striking thing, however, is how abstract, even within that partial focus, how obviously speculative, Rorty's thesis about the rescuers is. 'Perhaps', he suggests, they occasionally said something like this; but 'surely' they more often said something like that. These rescuers were real people and there is a body of writing about them, though in-depth study is mostly quite recent. An early piece is worth mentioning. In 1955, Philip Friedman, a pioneer of what is now called Holocaust research, published a short essay in which, after referring to rescuers who were activated by love, friendship, association through work or politics, he went on to speak also of the many whose motives were 'purely humanitarian' and who 'extended their help indiscriminately to all Jews in danger'. As a prime example of this latter kind of rescue, Friedman detailed some of the efforts made in different countries to save thousands of Jewish children.[5] He was writing, it is true, at a time when it was rarer than it is now for scholars of progressive outlook to put in question the viability of a 'universalistic attitude',[6] and his talk of purely humanitarian motives could be thought to be mere imputation, the construction of a pre-'post-modern' mind. But Friedman's example of the rescue of children may give one pause on this score.

Rescued children did not generally fall into such categories as 'comrade in the movement', 'fellow member of the same union or profession' or 'fellow bocce player'. They may, of course, have been fellow Milanese, Jutlanders, Belgians and the like, or even the children *of* fellow members of one parochial category or another. But it seems a nice point whether risking your life to save a child – or, as it was frequently, children – requires a more difficult act of sympathetic

11

identification than does taking that risk for a fellow Milanese, bocce player or whatever. In a book he published two years later, *Their Brothers' Keepers*, Philip Friedman told the story of another Maria, a Mother Maria. A Russian woman (born Elizabeth Pilenko) who had settled in France and become a nun in the Russian orthodox church, during the Nazi occupation she was at the centre of a clandestine organization rescuing Jews, amongst them many children. She was eventually captured and interrogated by the Gestapo. Her interrogator at one point put it to Mother Maria's mother, who was with her, that she had educated her daughter stupidly; the daughter only helped Jews. 'This is not true,' the old woman is said to have responded. 'She is a Christian who helps those in need. She would even help *you*, if you were in trouble.' Mother Maria died at Ravensbruck.[7]

I have no way of knowing, naturally, how well Mother Maria's mother understood her daughter's heart. But the story as told may suggest a counter-hypothesis to Rorty's. Children are only young humans. They are for a greater or lesser time dependent on adults, often vulnerable, a repository of hope and of much else. Can they not stand as a token in this context of the other routes to protective empathy there may be within the shared experience of human beings than just belonging to some smaller, exclusive community, whether concretized by locale and language, or functionally, or by political or religious belief? If the route may go via a child's vulnerability or its hope, or via the hope on its behalf, then so, surely, may it go via any person's anguish or desperate need; via any qualities indeed that transcend particular communities by being just common modes, so to say, of the human condition. But I may seem, now, to speculate in my own turn.

In neither his essay nor his book did Friedman give much in the way of direct quotation from rescuers themselves as to why they acted as they did. But his judgements were clearly based on a wide familiarity with actual cases throughout Europe and the sources of this familiarity were documented by him. On the other hand, what Rorty says on the subject gives every appearance of being only a casual example. There are reasons all the same, of both a general and a historically more specific kind, why his thesis may be seen by many as a plausible one. Generally, the theme of limited human altruism has a long pedigree already and there is enough evidence, goodness knows, of the realities which have inspired it. It has not just been confected out of thin air. Then, too, the taking of risks and making of sacrifices on behalf of other people plainly is often based on bonds of emotional or social contiguity. More specific to the cultural context in which we presently move is the fact that universalist viewpoints now sometimes get rather short shrift. Rorty demurs at having his ideas identified lock, stock and barrel with post-modernist thought,[8] but there is no doubt that what he has to say on this matter chimes in with anti-universalist philosophical attitudes which post-modernism has lately made fashionable. These seem to me to be good enough grounds for looking at his hypothesis in a serious way, mere casual example or not.

There is another reason for doing so. It concerns just what it was the rescuers did, what they are an example of. Although they tend in their own explanations to make little of what they did, treating it as the most obvious or natural thing, a simple duty and so on, the fact is that all around them others were acting otherwise. The rescuers present an example of uncommon generosity and moral courage in a murderous time, and it is not surprising if they assume for many writers the figure of heroes, a source of some redeeming optimism in a context yielding not very much of that.

Something should be said, as well, about the specific quality of their heroism, given the word's close association with military and, as it were, dragon-slaying exploits. While the stories of Jewish rescue do certainly include much that was extraordinary and dramatic, they also attest to a more mundane, resilient kind of heroism: drawn out and trying, burdened with the minutiae and costs of domestic life, a caring-for heroism, though not any less dangerous for that. It involved over long periods the getting and preparing of additional food, coping with extra laundry, having to carry away waste buckets from the hiding places to which those being sheltered were sometimes confined. And it involved just being, daily, at close quarters with them, attempting to maintain harmony under pressure. While strong affective ties between rescuers and rescued were often nurtured through the experiences they shared, people hidden could, like anybody else, turn out to be difficult or worse than difficult. In the words of one rescuer, 'Just because you have risked your life for somebody doesn't mean that that person is decent.'[9] For well-known reasons, and as male rescuers themselves emphasize, these burdens tended to fall more heavily on women, with men away from the house at work or otherwise out in the public domain, sometimes engaged in rescue and resistance activity elsewhere. They were burdens carried by individuals and families within an existence, as one Dutch scholar has put it, 'that was threatened every day, every hour, every minute'.[10] The penalties for sheltering Jews were extreme, often final. In Poland even the children of people caught doing so might not be spared.[11]

It seems at least incautious to draw advantage from this sort of moral example on the basis of no more than a 'surely'. Co-opting it willy-nilly to the side of one's argument is the less important aspect of the thing. The more important aspect is what that argument might then suggest about those who endured such risks on behalf of others. I don't want to get too heavy about this, but directly preceding Rorty's thesis on the rescuers and their reasons, a distinction is explicated by him (between 'us' and 'them') in terms of a notion of 'the wrong sort of human beings'. There are, of course, contexts where notions like that – 'another class of people', 'not my kind of folk' and so on – can be uttered more or less harmlessly or in a humanly understandable way. But Rorty's immediate context has to do with what reasons rescuers might have had for feeling that people in danger 'deserved to be saved'. If it is indeed true that most rescuers were moved by anti-universalist impulses, then this is something we need properly to register.

The real sources of their behaviour are certainly worth trying to understand, unobstructed by myth or mere phrases. On the other hand, *unless* it is true that they were moved by such impulses, Rorty's suggestion may unintentionally dishonour them.

II

Yad Vashem in Jerusalem, the Holocaust Martyrs' and Heroes' Remembrance Authority, has sought for more than three decades now, by a law of 1953 of the Israeli parliament, to identify and give due recognition to these people – under the honorific, 'Righteous Among the Nations'. This title is awarded on the basis of survivor testimony and other documentation, and each of those so recognized may plant a tree bearing his or her name on an avenue commemorating them all at Yad Vashem. The criteria which have evolved to cover the award are that it is for the carrying out of, or extending of aid in, an act of rescue; which was at personal risk; and without monetary reward.[12] To date more than nine thousand people have been recognized as 'Righteous Among the Nations', that figure not including the honour bestowed, exceptionally, on the Danish nation as a whole for its collective rescue of the Jews of Denmark.[13] Scholarly and more general interest in the recipients and in others like them (some of whom have declined to be honoured, disavowing any special virtue) has been slower to emerge. But there is now something of a literature on the subject. On several issues this literature – or such of it as I am familiar with, anyway – is inconclusive or not very illuminating. It can be reviewed, nevertheless, for what it does reveal.

There has been an interest in how far, if at all, rescuer behaviour can be related to differences of social position, gender, religious and political affiliation, family background, personal character and moral belief. To start with a local point, of the eleven hundred or so Jews who survived the war in hiding in Berlin, most, according to Yehuda Bauer, found

15

refuge in the working-class sections of the city. Moshe Bejski, who was a member of the Commission for the Designation of the Righteous, formed the more general impression from his years of work on it that, though rescuers came from all sectors of the population, the majority of them were from 'the lower classes'.[14] But there are also studies, on the other hand, including the two most thorough of recent works on this subject, that indicate a fairly even spread in terms of class and professional status. From her research on Polish rescuers, reported in her book *When Light Pierced the Darkness*, the sociologist Nechama Tec concluded that class was 'a weak predictor of Jewish rescue'. She found the numbers of both middle-class and working-class rescuers to be approximately par for the proportions of these two categories in the overall population; whilst, relative to their numbers, intellectuals were somewhat more, and peasants somewhat less, apt to give Jews shelter. Similarly, in *The Altruistic Personality*, a study of rescuers from several European countries, S.P. and P.M. Oliner report a quite even distribution in terms of occupational status. They suggest in this connection that 'economic resources . . . were not a critical factor influencing the decision to rescue'.[15]

In the essay I have already cited, Philip Friedman says that women, more easily moved emotionally than men, played an important role in rescue activity; and another author tells us that '[i]t was often women who were faced with the initial all-important decisions as to whether or not to take a stranger into their kitchens and into their homes . . .' The story of Maria Langthaler may come back to mind here. However, there are also studies of aid to German Jews from which it seems that fewer women than men may have been involved in it. In general there appears not to have been, as yet, enough detailed investigation of the gender aspects of this issue to enable any firm conclusions to be drawn.[16]

So it continues. According to Yehuda Bauer again, left-wing groups were on the whole inclined to help Jewish victims of Nazism. This is confirmed in some sort by Tec for the case of Polish rescuers: amongst those who were politically involved, most of the rescuers in her study were communists and socialists. On the other hand, the politically involved were themselves a minority relative to rescuers of no political affiliation – a pattern reported also by the Oliners from their wider study. And Tec records non-leftists as well, albeit a minority, amongst her politically affiliated rescuers. The Oliners' categorization is different here but implies a smaller proportion (amongst the 'political' rescuers) specifically of the left: of the minority of rescuers in their study who were politically affiliated (21 per cent), the majority belonged to democratic parties, not distinguished as between left and other, but only a minority of them to parties described as of the 'economic left'.[17]

As for religion, the research all points toward the same broad picture. Many rescuers were religious, and many rescuers were not. They were devout Christians of all denominations, people of a more general, less attached kind of faith, humanists, atheists. Because of long-standing traditions of anti-semitism within it, Christianity could dispose its adherents against helping Jews – though a few anti-semites did help, their prejudices notwithstanding – and, through its ethical teachings, it could also dispose them towards helping Jews. There is some consensus, in fact, amongst researchers that it was the moral content of religious teaching that was primary with most of the rescuers who do cite their religion as a central motivating impulse.[18]

An interim observation may perhaps be made before we proceed further. The findings so far summarized confirm an impression gained from more general, popular accounts of rescue activity. In one sense, obviously, there were too few rescuers. They made up a very small proportion of the European populations to which they belonged. However, there were enough of them in each of the categories we have been considering – enough women and men, enough workers, peasants, middle-class people and intellectuals, enough believers and non-believers, enough communists and liberals – and there were, *a fortiori*, enough non-rescuers as well within the same categories, for the question under discussion here to be pertinent across all the categories. What were the reasons of those (men, women, intellectuals, Christians, etc.) who risked their lives?[19]

The existing research has also concerned itself with other, broadly characterological, kinds of indicator. It has sought to discover if there might be clues to the rescuers' conduct in the temperaments, types of personality or childhood influences discernible amongst them. An early study, not completed owing to lack of funds, has been influential in directing subsequent researchers towards certain questions. In an essay published in 1970, Perry London reported three impressions derived from his unfinished study: a significant sense amongst the rescuers interviewed of being socially marginal, of standing at odds with or apart from the surrounding community in some way; then, a spirit of adventurousness, evident from the lives of many of them even prior to their rescue activity; finally, an intense identification with a parental model of moral conduct – with no apparent pattern, here, relating to gender.[20] Later work, by Douglas Huneke, and by Samuel Oliner (as relayed by him in articles preceding the *Altruistic Personality* study aforementioned), supported London on the finding of social marginality; as did Nechama Tec's book, though under the description she preferred of 'separateness' or 'individuality', in which she merged London's categories of social marginality and adventurousness.[21] Others too (Huneke, Samuel Oliner, Coopersmith) have fallen in with London's impressions on adventurousness – or at any rate 'confidence' – as they have on the strong parental moral influence as well.[22]

However, there are contrary indications once again, most strongly with regard to social marginality. In a study of Dutch rescuers Lawrence Baron did not find a high proportion of socially marginal individuals; and this result is repeated across several countries by the latest and most comprehensive Oliner study, which thereby contradicts his own earlier suggestions on the point. The finding of *The Altruistic Personality* is that 'the overwhelming majority of rescuers (80 percent) had a sense of belonging to their community', a proportion which was almost identical to that found in the comparative sample of non-rescuers.[23]

As to London's other two tentative impressions, although there is no precise or detailed data to set against them so far as I am aware, there are certainly counter-impressions – and from writers as well placed in terms of their knowledge of actual cases. Tec, whose other findings, as we have seen, agree with London's, demurs over just how general among rescuers was the identification with parental values. The family could, but also need not, be the reference point. Rescuers' values sometimes originated independently, from religious or political sources. And Mordecai Paldiel at Yad Vashem, who is sceptical of these correlations in their entirety, puts in question both the generalization about parental identification and that about adventurousness and the like. For each generalization, as for most such, he argues, there are counter-examples aplenty to go with the many examples.[24] With respect to these two generalizations, in any case, it seems appropriate to ask what we would have discovered even were they to be confirmed. It could hardly be surprising if people who took great risks on behalf of others did score higher on 'adventurousness' or 'confidence' than people at large. (It should be registered though, at the same time, that most rescuers do not present themselves as fearless or inordinately bold. From what they say, they had just the sort of feelings you and I can imagine having in a situation of grave risk.) Equally, since one important source of moral education clearly is parental influence, it should not be too startling if a fair to good proportion of the Righteous do profess something like the identification reported by Perry London. The same, I think, goes for the finding of Douglas Huneke that rescuers in his study came out well on 'hospitality'.[25]

How common was it for rescuers to be acquainted – as friends, lovers, neighbours, colleagues – with the Jews they helped? I have not found a precise answer to this question and it is unlikely anybody knows it. Because people do often go out of their way for those they like or love, cherish, and so on, one would expect there to have been such cases in significant number, and there were. They are emphasized in some of this literature. In his earlier articles, Samuel Oliner focuses on them, both in summarizing Coopersmith's uncompleted work and on his own behalf. He estimates that perhaps as many as 75 per cent of those rescued were previously known to their rescuers or belonged to the same social network as they did. Reporting this estimate Lawrence Baron, too, encourages the inference that prior relationship may have been the more typical case. But Baron himself cites a study (by Wolfson) according to which, in a group of Germans who helped Jews between 1938 and 1945, only a few had been friends with those they saved.[26] And in general the notion that prior relationship was the most frequent case seems to have been formed impressionistically. Where there are specific data – and from studies involving hundreds of both rescuers and rescued – the picture comes out different.

In Nechama Tec's Polish study, a minority of the Jews rescued reported having been helped by friends. More than half were protected by strangers: 51 per cent, as compared with 19 and 30 per cent, respectively, by friends and acquaintances. Similarly, a minority of her rescuers helped only friends; an 'overwhelming majority' helped total strangers or mere acquaintances, the distribution strongly tilted towards the former. The Oliners' *Altruistic Personality* project reveals the same thing: 'More than half had no pre-war acquaintance with any of the Jews they helped. Almost 90 percent helped at least one Jewish stranger.'[27] Even in terms of more general familiarity and contact, these two studies indicate large numbers of rescuers without previous ties with Jews. According to the Oliners, more than 40 per cent of their rescuers had no Jewish friends, and more than 65 per cent no Jewish co-workers. Of Tec's rescuers 20 per cent had no ties of any kind with Jews.[28] It is not perhaps surprising in the light of all this that Tec should say about the attitude prevailing amongst them, 'Anyone in need qualified for help.'[29]

Or is it surprising? For we are brought back by this to the hypothesis with which we began. Richard Rorty, we saw, reckons on the likelihood of parochial identifications and commitments having been more typical than universalist ones amongst people who risked their lives on behalf of Jews. Others may well reckon otherwise. They may reckon that universalist commitments are exactly what you would expect to find amongst them. However this may be, here finally we do come upon something on which there is near unanimity in the literature under review. In an area of research where, as I have tried to show, the findings are very various, at odds with one another, inconclusive; or else are just indicative of a diversity of rescuer belief, as on religion – in this area the commentators speak with respect to one point in practically one voice. It is a universalist voice.

Moshe Bejski believes 'the humanitarian motivation which dictates a charitable attitude toward one's fellow man' to have been dominant amongst the numerous considerations that moved rescuers. Andre Stein concludes his book about Dutch rescuers, 'what [they] seem to have in common is a direct link with their fellow humans, regardless of who those humans are. They see the suffering, and . . . they take action.' From a study of French Catholics who aided Jews, Eva Fleischner could isolate no single common motive other than 'the conviction, shared by all, that Jews must be helped because they were victims' – 'fellow human beings in need'. Kristen Monroe and her co-authors found amongst the rescuers they interviewed a 'perception of themselves as one with all humankind', 'part of a shared humanity'. In connection with parental models of moral conduct, Douglas Huneke refers to the religious teachings and 'humanistic perspectives' imparted to the rescuers he interviewed. 'They had been taught', he says, 'to value other human beings.' Or they knew, as he also says, how to contain their prejudices, and he gives a sort of limit case of this, of a rescuer who believed that the Jews may

21

have brought their suffering upon themselves: by declining to forsake Judaism for Christianity; because they had crucified the Christ; and so forth. Shocked by the suggestion that her views might be seen as a justification of Nazi aims, this woman went on to say, 'But the Jews are human beings. No one has the right to kill people because of what they believe.'[30]

Samuel Oliner, even in the earlier articles highlighting cases of people with a prior social link to those they helped, does not neglect to pick out as one of several key motives amongst rescuers, 'their love of humanity'. He speaks of them, also, as having been reared in an environment emphasizing 'a universal sense of justice'. Subsequently, he and Pearl Oliner report the finding of their *Altruistic Personality* study, that a large majority of rescuers emphasized the ethical meaning for them of the help they gave: some of these in terms of the value of equity or fairness; more of them in terms of the value of care; but in any case with a sense of responsibility common amongst them that was 'broadly inclusive in character, extending to all human beings'. In fact, the Oliners' figures give half of all rescuers as owning to 'a universalistic view of their ethical obligations' – this as compared with 15 per cent moved by a desire to assist friends. Nechama Tec, for her part, gives as many as 95 per cent of rescuers from her study as ascribing their decision to help to simple 'compassion for Jewish suffering' (against 36 per cent to bonds of friendship and 27 per cent to religious convictions). They displayed, she says, a 'universalistic perception of the needy'. And Mordecai Paldiel postulates an innate human altruism which, weakened by societal influences of one kind and another, can be suddenly activated 'in order to uphold the principle of the sanctity of life'.[31]

I now propose two more – although competing – hypotheses. I shall call them the 'naive' hypothesis and the 'sceptical' hypothesis. Each responds differently to the question of what one is to make of the broad consensus just documented. The naive hypothesis, which is mine, is this. If so many who are familiar with actual rescuers concur on this one point regarding the motives prevalent amongst them, it is likely to be because a 'universalistic attitude' was indeed general, contrary to Rorty's speculation. The commentators' judgements so to say mirror the explanations of the people about whom those judgements are made. The sceptical hypothesis, on the other hand, I construct merely by anticipation, and it is as follows. Well, of course, this is just what the commentators *would* say – in an intellectual culture saturated by universalist grand narratives, essentialist concepts of 'human nature' and the like.[32]

We need perhaps, then, to give some attention to the voice of the rescuers themselves. That is what I next undertake.

III

I have not, it should at once be said, interviewed any of the people about to make an appearance here. I have only read of them. Nevertheless, if from the literature I have managed to consult one leaves aside a certain volume of quotation not attributed to specific individuals, a sample of several dozen rescuers can be assembled, all of them identified by name, who tell something of their stories and something of their reasons.[33] Obviously, this assembly is not governed by any scientific sampling method. I tread, possibly, on thin ice. But I venture to say all the same that, unless by a freak chance an altogether odd collection of rescuers has been thrown before me, the naive hypothesis looks pretty good. I will go further. It is not very easy to find people – from some eighty of them – who say the sort of thing, or at any rate just the sort of thing, that Rorty surmises rescuers usually said.

Here are Arnold Douwes and Seine Otten, two close friends interviewed together. They were part of a network of people in the town of Nieuwlande in the Netherlands, who provided shelter to hundreds of Jews. Otten recalls his wife's saying, 'we should try to save as many as we can'. In fact, she and he hid fifty Jews in all during the period of the Nazi occupation.

23

Douwes, though not himself Jewish, was arrested early on for wearing the yellow star. His role in rescue activity came to include attending to the many needs of Jews in hiding – for food, money, false papers and so on – and searching the countryside to find people willing to take them in. 'It wasn't a question', he says, 'of why we acted. The question is why things weren't done by others. You could do nothing else; it's as simple as that. It was obvious. When you see injustice done you do something against it. When you see people being persecuted, and I didn't care whether they were Jews or Eskimos or Catholics or whatever, they were persecuted people and you had to help them.'[34]

Here is John Weidner. A Dutch businessman working in France during the war, he helped escort hundreds of Jews to safety in Switzerland, travelling on skis across the mountains. Involved in the same rescue organization, his sister was caught and killed by the Nazis. Weidner himself was tortured, suffering a permanent impairment of his speech. On one occasion, at the station in Lyon, he witnessed an SS officer crushing the head of a Jewish infant under his boot. Weidner says that what the Nazis did went against everything he was taught to believe; they 'had no respect for [the] human dignity' of the Jews. A Seventh-Day Adventist, he speaks of 'his concept of love and compassion', of the need 'to have a heart open to the suffering of others'. He says: 'I hope God will know I did the best I could to help people.'[35]

Such sentiments are not unusual in my quasi-sample of rescuers, they are typical. Eva Anielska, a Polish woman, a socialist and member of Zegota – the underground Council of Aid to Jews that was active in Poland from late 1942 on – helped save many people, most of them strangers. 'One saw the Jew', she says, 'not as a Jew, but as a persecuted human being, desperately struggling for life and in need of help . . . a persecuted, humiliated human being . . .' Jorgen Kieler was a member of the Danish Resistance Movement. Ascribing to the Danish people 'a traditional humanistic attitude to life', he says: 'National independence and democracy were our common goals, but the persecution of the Jews added a new and overwhelming dimension to the fight against Hitler: human rights. Our responsibility toward and our respect for the individual human being became the primary goals of the struggle.' Kieler mentions also the German official, Georg Duckwitz. Duckwitz was at the time shipping attaché at the German legation in Copenhagen. He warned his Danish contacts when the deportation of the Jews was about to begin, so making a decisive contribution to the collective rescue that followed. When the risk he had taken was later pointed out to him, he responded, 'Everyone should see himself in the situation in which he, too, like his fellow man, might find himself.'[36]

Bill and Margaret Bouwma sheltered on their farm in turn a woman, a teenage girl who was murdered by Dutch Nazis when she was out one day on her own, and then another girl. Induced by a question from the woman to ponder just why he was doing what he was, Bill Bouwma answered: because he was brought up always to help the weak; because he knew what it felt like to be the underdog; because his faith taught him to open his door to the homeless, the refugee – and, more simply, because a voice inside him said he had to do it, otherwise he would no longer be himself. Margaret Bouwma told one of the girls, 'It's not that we are friends of the Jews or their enemies. It is our human duty to open our home . . . and our hearts to anyone who suffers.' Another Dutch couple, Rudy and Betty de Vries, hid a family of three not previously known to them and then others as well in the home above their butcher shop; and Rudy was involved more generally in underground and rescue activity. Betty felt at times overwhelmed by the extra work, but convinced herself 'that it was a very small price to pay for saving three lives'. Rudy reports a sympathetic encounter with a German soldier in the shop. He says that many 'failed to see the man in their enemy', but 'Jews or Germans – it made no difference to me, as long as I could see them as human beings.' When first approached to shelter people, he hesitated only a moment; he had been

taught as a child to distinguish between justice and injustice. 'My faith', he says, 'commands . . . me to love my fellow man, without exclusions.'[37]
One repeatedly comes across instances, in fact, of Perry London's sort of rescuer: people who cite a strong parental influence in speaking about the help they gave. A German engineer, Hermann Graebe – known also for some terrible, heart-breaking testimony concerning an episode he witnessed during the mass shooting of the Jews of Dubno – saved the lives of dozens of Jews working under his management in eastern Poland. 'I believe that my mother's influence on me when I was a child has a lot to do with it . . . She told me . . . that I should not take advantage of other people's vulnerability . . . She said, "Take people as they come – not by profession, not by religion, but by what they are as persons."' Mihael Mihaelov, a Bulgarian, tells that both his parents were of very generous disposition. Mihaelov hid property for many Jews and brought food to them in the labour camps. He had seen Germans beating Jews and breaking their bones. 'I don't know exactly why I helped. It's just the kind of person I am. When I see someone who needs help I help them, and my whole family is like that.' In the town of Topusko on the Bosnian border in Yugoslavia, Ivan Vranetic helped and hid many Jews fleeing from the Nazis. The first of them was a man who approached him in desperate straits: 'He had no shoes, nothing, and when he started to tell me his story I had to help him. I think it must be in my upbringing . . .' Vranetic says that his father 'liked people no matter what religion they were' and his mother was a good woman; 'we were brought up to love humankind.'[38]
I interject now a first sceptical question on behalf of anyone who is wary vis-à-vis my naive hypothesis. The question might go like this: as what is here documented so far are the explanations put forward by rescuers many years after the events to which their explanations relate, how good a guide can these be to their motives at the time? How indicative is what they say now of what they felt, what really moved them, then?

There are a number of things one can offer in response to this question. First, since what I report these rescuers as saying is what rescuers seem to say, not just here or there, but quite generally and consistently, is it not likely to tell us something about what they actually felt at the time? Or must we rather suppose on the part of all these people a systematic – a common – misconstrual of their own reasons? Second, what they now say quite generally and consistently seems likely on the face of it to be as good a guide to their reasons as anything imputed to them on the basis merely of a current philosophical commitment. Third, one can try also to discover what was said by such people *then*. The evidence I have been able to gather about this suggests it might not have been all that different from what they say now.

A young French Catholic, Germaine Ribière, in the period before anyone in the Church hierarchy in France had spoken out against the persecution of the Jews there, committed her feelings about this to the diary she kept. 'I ache for them in my whole being, I ache for my Jewish brothers and sisters,' she writes when seven thousand Polish Jews are rounded up in Paris; and then, after she has visited two internment camps, 'Total contempt for the human being.' She speaks to a rabbi, saying she will help in any way she can. Another entry by her reads, 'Humanity is the body of Christ. One part of that humanity is being tortured . . . And we look on in silence as the crime is being perpetrated.' (Today, incidentally, Ribière tells her interviewer also, 'My mother raised us to have respect for life.') When finally a small number of bishops do break their silence, what do they say? They speak the same sort of language as Germaine Ribière. The Archbishop of Toulouse, Jules Gérard Saliège, writes in a letter of August 1942, 'it has been destined for us to witness the dreadful spectacle of children, women and old men being treated like vile beasts . . . The Jews are our brethren. They belong to mankind.' A few days later in a letter to be read within his diocese, the Bishop of Montauban, Pierre-Marie Théas, similarly proclaims, 'all men . . . are brothers, because they are created by the same

God . . . all, whatever their race or religion, are entitled to respect . . . The current anti-semitic measures are in contempt of human dignity.'[39] That was then. When therefore, now, another woman, Marie-Rose Gineste, who spent four days on her bicycle delivering Monsignor Théas's letter and then took charge at his request of the hiding of the Jews of Montauban, says, 'It was all about human justice . . .', how plausible actually is it to suppose she would have expressed herself very differently at the time?[40] Or we may take the example of Pieter Miedema. He was a minister in the Dutch Reformed Church in Friesland. As he has been incapacitated by a stroke, his wife, Joyce, now speaks for him. The Miedemas hid Jews in their own home, and he, the minister, was also active in finding hiding places for them elsewhere in the area. He had to go on the run at one point in order to avoid arrest or worse. Pieter Miedema has declined to be honoured by Yad Vashem, having done only 'what everyone should have done'. Joyce Miedema now construes his thinking so: 'if you opt against opening your home and heart to an innocent fugitive, you have no place in the community of the just'; you choose 'the worst solitude a man can discover: his own exclusion from the family of man'. One might be tempted to take this for a merely second-hand sentiment – except that it was part of a sermon given by Miedema at the time, which his wife says will stay in her mind always, 'word for word'.[41]

Or, again, there is the example of Zofia Kossak-Szczucka. A Catholic author and right-wing nationalist, she wrote a leaflet protesting against the murder of the Jews of Poland and helped to found Zegota, the organization for aiding them. She was caught and sent to Auschwitz where she spent nearly a year. On her release, she became active in the rescue of Jewish children. Szczucka's writings of the period give expression both to some anti-semitic convictions and to an energetic appeal on behalf of the Polish Jews. In one piece, she writes that after the war they will be told, 'Go and settle somewhere else.' But now they 'are the victims of unjust murderous

persecutions' and 'Christ stands behind every human
being . . . He stretches His hand to us through a runaway Jew
from the ghetto the same way as He does through our brothers.' In the protest leaflet, Jews are described by her as the
'enemies of Poland'; but also as 'condemned people' and
'defenceless people', 'insane from grief and horror'. Their
present plight Szczucka calls 'your fellow man's calamity'.[42]
That also was then. Today, another Polish Catholic writer
and anti-semite, Marek Dunski, explains himself as follows.
His motivation arose from his religious convictions. 'One
could not simply allow a person to die.' In wartime, he says,
evidently generalizing from his own case, people recur to more
basic things: 'They tend to see a person as a human being.
This is what happened with the Jews. They were not seen as
Jews but as human beings.' Or the individual Jew was seen
simply as 'a hurt, suffering being'. Dunski speaks as well, in
connection with the aid he brought to a threatened Russian
soldier, of not having 'any special fondness for Russians', yet
of feeling 'that a human being ought to be saved at any price'.
Marek Dunski had a part in the rescue of several hundred
Jewish children. His reasons as given do not strike me as any
less to be relied on for having been articulated later than
Szczucka's similar ones.[43]

Some readers may be starting to wonder, secondly, why the
material I have cited does not reflect (what we know to be the
case from the review of literature in the previous section) that
there were rescuers who helped their friends. It does not
reflect it yet. Only because I have not got there yet. I was
coming to them. Here is one category of such rescuers.

Bert Bochove and his first wife Annie (now deceased) hid a
friend of Annie's when she came and asked for help. They
then also hid thirty-six other people. Bochove says, 'it was
easy to do because it was your duty', 'I got such satisfac-
tion . . . from keeping people safe' and 'You help people
because you are human and you see that there is a need.'[44]
Tina Strobos's family, social democrats and atheists, hid Tina's
best friend who was Jewish. The family had a tradition of

helping others – refugees, miners' children. During the war they hid about a hundred people, though never more than five at a time: 'Some we knew, some we didn't.' Strobos says she believes in 'the sacredness of life'; today she gives talks to schoolchildren and tells them 'we have to be careful not to hurt others who don't belong to our little group.'[45]

Zofia Baniecka for her part would like children to know that there were people in Poland like Tina Strobos. Baniecka herself and her mother hid or found hiding places for Jews escaping from the Warsaw ghetto. One of these was a school friend – 'so of course I didn't turn her away'. But, as Baniecka also says, 'We hid at least fifty Jews during the war – friends, strangers, acquaintances, or someone who heard about me from someone else. Anyone was taken in.' Baniecka says she 'believe[s] in human beings'.[46] And then Jan Elewski. A Polish officer and leftist who protected his best friend from anti-semitic persecution before the war, he also saved seven strangers during the war by moving them to a more secure hiding place and supplying them with food there. He speaks of a 'feeling of duty' by contrast with the self-centredness of others who did not help; and of the thought that his family would have disowned him for 'not helping people who were being destroyed'. And Roman Sadowski also. He was a member of Zegota. He tried desperately to contact Jewish friends in the Warsaw ghetto when the deportations to the death camps began, but he failed and they perished. He then gave aid mostly to strangers: 'whoever turned to me, and whomever I could find'. Why? 'Their being Jewish did not play a part at all. Regardless of who they were, needing help was the criteria [sic] . . . Human life was at stake.'[47]

And Jean Kowalyk Berger. And Ada Celka. In the Ukrainian village in which the former lived, the Germans set up a labour camp and she saw there 'the cruelty . . . day after day'. She and her family agreed to hide a Jewish doctor who had earlier helped her. He arrived one night at their door, begging to be taken in. 'Then more people came during that night . . . If you could have seen my house . . . Everything was so difficult.' She describes how difficult. When she is asked why she helped, she says, 'When I saw people being molested, my religious heart whispered to me, "Don't kill. Love others as you love yourself."' Ada Celka, deeply religious as well, living in poverty in a one-room apartment with her sister and disabled father, took in the daughter of a Jewish friend. Herself a Pole, she also sheltered Russian partisans. 'What I did was everybody's duty. Saving the one whose life is in jeopardy is a simple human duty. One has to help another regardless of who this human being is as long as he is in need, that is all that counts.'[48]

It seems not uncommon amongst the Righteous: people who help friends or acquaintances and who help people other than friends or acquaintances, help people who are strangers to them; and who give universalizing reasons for doing what they do. About people like them it would seem safe to conclude that those reasons are not then merely rhetorical superstructures on or rationalizing derivations from friendship – as the putative 'real' cause (or essence) of rescuer behaviour. What, however, of rescuers whose help was just for friends? Or just for friends and the relations of friends? Or whose help was primarily such? Here at least, it might seem clear, we would have come upon the Rorty sort of rescuer. I suggest, on the contrary, that that is not so clear. Let us consider first in this connection the story of Irene Opdyke.

Opdyke was a student nurse at the time of the invasion of Poland. She speaks of her mother as a strong influence – 'she never turned away anyone from her doorstep', 'always knew how to help' – and speaks of her own vocation to be a nurse likewise in terms of helping people. Opdyke was beaten and raped by Russian soldiers and later impressed into labour by the Nazis. Running an errand one day in the nearby ghetto she witnessed scenes of great brutality. 'Most of all, I remember the children', she says. Opdyke decided that 'if the opportunity arrived I would help these people.' She subsequently befriended twelve Jews employed in the laundry at her place of work. As she puts it, 'I didn't have a family. They were persecuted. It was a human bond.' When she then learned of a move impending to liquidate the ghetto, she managed to hide and finally save these friends, at a not insignificant personal cost to herself. She says 'that we belong all together. That no matter what a person's colour, race, religion, or language, we are created by one God'; and that 'all human beings belong to one . . . family.'[49]

Did Irene Opdyke save her friends only because they were her friends? Or did she save them because of the moral commitments she tried to live by, of the kind of person she was? Or: what was the balance between her feelings of friendship and her more general values or moral impulses, in moving her to act on behalf of people threatened? This question, actually, does not seem all that interesting in relation to Opdyke herself. She plainly had enough reasons, and good ones, to act as she did; and since she herself lays emphasis upon reasons of both kinds, who else could presume to say exactly what the balance was between them? But the question of the balance, of the interrelationship between different sorts of reason, does not closely depend, as it happens, on the chronology or details of Opdyke's particular story. It is of much broader applicability. For it would seem to be the case with those rescuers who came to the aid of friends, acquaintances and other such connected folk, that they also will generally explain themselves in the way we have begun to be familiar with, giving expression to universalist commitments. They – also – say the kind of thing that Rorty suggests rescuers would not usually have said.

Hela Horska, a doctor's wife, who hid the young son of one of her husband's patients and eventually thirteen other members of his family as well, says: 'All my life I worked for social causes . . . It did not matter who it was if someone needed help I had to give it . . . I helped because a human being ought to help another.' Albert and Wilma Dijkstra sheltered people Albert knew from his home town. The Dijkstras speak in terms of hiding 'Jewish friends . . . in danger' – and also of their belief 'that life is sacred', of their 'concern [having] always been with human life and not to whom it belongs', of not 'distinguishing [in this regard] between Christian and Jew, German and Dutch'. Gitta Bauer, who hid a family friend, says it was not a big decision: 'She was a friend and she needed help.' Bauer also says that her father had taught her, 'Jews are people like you and me only with a different religion. And that's it.' She has always been 'concerned about racism of any kind'. Libuse Fries brought aid to a workmate (her husband-to-be) in Theresienstadt, and she helped his sister also and was imprisoned for doing so. Fries was brought up, she tells, 'to love nature and all human beings'; she 'thought it was inhuman to take young people from their families for no reason'. Germaine Belline and Liliane Gaffney, a mother and daughter, helped many Jewish friends: two brothers, their sister, her children, a niece, 'cousins of cousins'. They say: it felt 'natural' because these were friends; and '[t]he one thing I could never stand as a child is injustice'; and 'if you didn't live for others . . . it wasn't worth living. To be human we need each other.'[50]

And one 'Stanislaus' who had Jewish friends in the Warsaw ghetto nearby, and who together with his mother gave out much help, to friends and others – soup, shelter, finding hideouts. His reasons: 'Human compassion.' And Louise Steenstra who lost her husband, killed in their home by German soldiers for hiding a Jewish friend. She and her husband could not be 'insensitive', she remembers, to the fate looming over the various friends they helped: 'we felt so sorry for those Jewish people with their kids screaming when the Nazis came in the night to pick them up'; '[w]hen you are the mother of one child, you are mother to them all'.[51] And Gustav Mikulai who, 'see[ing] poverty and injustice all around [him]', became a social democrat in his youth, and who all his life has 'had three passions: music, women and Jews' – one of whom he married. He hid his wife and in-laws, and indeed together with a friend 'all the Jews we could'. He was 'sort of drunk with [his] rebellion against the horrible injustice' to them. 'It was a terrible time for humanity.' And Orest Zahajkewycz and Helena Melnyczuk, brother and sister, who hid friends in their home and whose father 'was always trying to help somebody', and who have tried to teach their own children 'to be human' and do the same. They also recall that period, by contrast, in terms of its 'horror – that one human being could do this to another.'[52]

And then, to finish with this grouping in my quasi-sample of rescuers, there is Stefania Podgorska Burzminski. She gave refuge in her apartment to the son of a Jewish woman she worked for, and later to his brother and his sister-in-law; in all, to thirteen people and 'for two winters'. Pivotal to her story as she tells it is this:

> Before the war everyone shopped and talked together and everything was fine. But then there was the segregation and the mark of the Jewish star, and that was confusing for me. One day I saw a Jewish boy on the street, about nine years old, and another boy came up to him and said, 'You are a Jew!' and he hit him. A man, just an ordinary worker, saw it and said, 'Why would you do that? He's a boy just like you. Look at his hands, his face. There's no difference. We have enemies now from another country who say there's a difference, but there isn't.' So the boy who hit the Jewish boy looked sad and said, 'Oh, all right, I'm sorry.' I listened to him and I came home and I looked at my hands and I said, 'No, there is no difference.' So, you see, I listened and I learned.

Learned just about helping fellow denizens of Poland perhaps? Today, Podgorska voices a concern with the need to 'teach people humanity'.[53]

Now, it might be suggested that with rescuers whose aid was (or was primarily) to people more or less closely connected to them, the articulation of universalist motives and humanist principles *can* be discounted. They helped whom they knew, you see, and everything else would be at best well-meaning sentiment. But for my own part I do not see how this could possibly be asserted with any confidence, much less explanatory authority. That someone is a friend is in itself, of course, a perfectly good reason for helping them. On the other hand, the pertinent context here is one in which an inestimably large number of people precisely did not help friends, neighbours and other acquaintances. They stood by, looked on or turned away, whether in fear or shame or merely with indifference, as the Jews they knew were taken away or fled. In that sense, as a matter of ethico-sociological generalization, friendship or familiarity plainly is not a sufficient condition of one person's coming to the aid of another in serious jeopardy. If against this background so many of the rescuers who gave help to people close to them tell universalizing stories about what they did and who they are, as well as or sometimes rather than citing friendship and the like, on what basis can it be claimed that their universalizing stories vouchsafe us nothing of what 'really' impelled them?

It might now in turn be said, though, that this reasoning can be reversed against me. How many people also, it will be pointed out, professing similar moral viewpoints to all these rescuers, did not bring aid to Jews in danger. It is, again, an inestimably large number. The argument does not discomfit me, however, nor is the case so reversed genuinely symmetrical with the one it supposedly reverses. For I do not seek to belittle or minimize the part which might have been played by friendship and other particularist loyalties in contributing to individuals' motives for rescue. I simply meet here the effort to belittle or minimize the part played by universalist moral attachments, setting down what I have found. Nor does setting it down imply any claim that, as a matter of ethico-sociological generalization, universal moral attachments might on their part be a sufficient condition of rescue. The point is only that it is a complicated question just what combination of reasons, motives and other factors – temperamental, situational and so on – does, and just what combination does not, move people to act under risk for other

35

people; a question to which no one, so far as I know, has the answer, if indeed there is *an* answer. All I do is report that a universalist moral outlook appears to have had a very significant part in motivating Jewish rescue. Many rescuers give voice to it and few do not. At the same time, no rescuer I have come across overtly repudiates it. To be sure, there were such people about also, at that time. They seem not to have been heavily involved in helping Jews is all. We know what some of them were doing.

A third and last query on behalf of the sceptical: Are there, then, no rescuers within my sample who are of that sort who say 'fellow Milanese . . . fellow Jutlander'? In fact, only one case I have been able to discover perhaps fits here. It is a Dane, unnamed in the source in which I find him, who says, 'The main reason I did it was because I didn't want anybody to hurt my friends, my neighbours, my fellow countrymen, without cause.' Even he makes some additional remarks as well, of seemingly broader scope, but ambiguously so. I mark him down as one for Richard Rorty anyway. This Dane is (if he is) a rare figure in the present company.[54]

It is another case, rather, that captures what seems to be the more general situation with rescuers who refer to their communities. Aart and Johtje Vos gave shelter in their home near Amsterdam to many who needed it, at one time hiding more than thirty Jews as well as a few other people. She, Johtje, says: 'We never talked about Jews [in Holland]. They were all just Dutch, that's all.' And he, Aart, says: 'Holland was like a family and part of that family was in danger. In this case, the Jewish part. The Germans were threatening our family.' This seems clear enough. But there is more. Aart Vos also recounts how one day after a bombing he found a wounded German soldier and helped him back to his camp. Asked by friends how he could bring himself to 'save a German', he replied, 'My wife and I were brought up to have respect for life.' Johtje Vos, relating the same incident elsewhere, puts it that their friends reproached Aart with helping the enemy and that his response to them was, 'No, the moment the man was badly wounded, he was not an enemy anymore but simply a human being in need.' And, this episode aside, Aart and Johtje Vos, looking beyond themselves and their children, that is, beyond their own family to a wider Dutch 'family', patently look further still. Johtje says that both she and Aart were brought up not to be prejudiced on grounds of 'race, colour, creed, nationality, or whatever . . . so it came very naturally to us to consider Jews just like us. We thought of them as human beings, just as we were.' Your response in that situation, she also says, depends on 'the result of your upbringing, your character, on your general love for people . . .' Again: 'We helped people who were in need. Who they were was absolutely immaterial to us. It wasn't that we were especially fond of Jewish people. We felt we wanted to help everybody who was in trouble.' During the war, Aart says, he 'thought it wasn't possible that on this little planet people could do [the sort of things they did] to each other'.[55]

Just as friendship, as we have seen, need not be the only reason of someone who goes to the aid of a friend, so a commitment to compatriots, fellow citizens or other locally specific communities does not have to exclude more general humanitarian concern. With the rescuers the common pattern would seem to be that it did not. And is this so surprising? Mutual loyalty or solidarity within such communities can, it is true, be of an exclusionary sort; or it may sometimes simply relate to matters in which a more extensive identification would not be – for *those* matters – appropriate. It is also the case, however, that a person who says 'Dutch, just like us', 'fellow Dane' and so forth, may be appealing to a notion of civic equality and reciprocal obligation closely tied, as a matter of historical and cultural fact, to wider egalitarian, humanistic, universalist values. Especially when what is at stake is a matter of life, death or grave suffering, to think, 'Dutch like the rest of us', may only be to think, 'Another *person* in the Dutch community'. It need not be very different from thinking, 'Fellow human being'.

Such, at any rate, commonly was the case with the rescuers. Like Aart and Johtje Vos, those of them who allude to
the specificities of community invariably point beyond these
as well. Marion Pritchard who had a part in saving more
than a hundred Jews says, 'In Holland, the Jews were considered Dutch like everyone else.' She learned tolerance from
her father, 'more accepting of all people and their differences
than my mother', and was imbued early on 'with a strong
conviction that we are our brothers' keepers'. Decisive for
Pritchard was the experience of happening to witness Nazis
loading, throwing – 'by an arm, a leg, the hair' – young children, taken from a Jewish children's home, on to trucks. 'To
watch grown men treat small children that way . . . I found
myself literally crying with rage.' Pritchard's words do not, to
me, encourage the inference that it was the 'Dutchness' of
these victims that was for her the key thing.[56]

In turn, a certain 'Johan' explains himself so: 'The main
reason was because I was a patriot. I was for my country.'
He continues: 'The Germans robbed people of their freedom. And when they started taking the Jewish people, that
really lit my fire . . . I really became full of hate because they
took innocent people – especially when they took little kids.
That was the worst.' This same 'Johan' says he learned from
his parents that 'Jews were just people'. His mother would
never 'look down' on anyone. 'She would always appreciate
what people were worth.' And then John and Bertha Datema
recall some of their wartime reactions. John: that 'those
people are Dutch, Jewish or not, they are Dutch'; and that 'I
had witnessed more human suffering than I could cope
with.' And Bertha: 'Every wasted life is another nail in
Christ's body. When a child is destroyed, all of us become
orphans.' And Helene Jacobs, a German rescuer for whom
'A community which destroys a part of itself on purpose, out
of hatred, gives itself up. It degenerates. This happened in
our country.' Jacobs explains her own rescue work like this:
'They were people who were in danger and I wanted to help
them. It was as simple as that.' And like this: 'I always knew

how dangerous it was, but I did it for humanity, and because I was a patriot.'[57]

Who here, once again, can claim to know the exact balance of these rescuers' reasons: between community, country or patriotism on the one hand; and humanity; children; people in danger or trouble or need, on the other? I have now given, in any event, some account of rather more than half of the rescuers in my sample. Considerations both of space and for the patience of the reader deter me from relating, even in the truncated and reduced forms I have had to adopt for the stories I have told, the other stories remaining. But the stories left untold tell just the same story as the stories told. I let the subjects of them, of the ones I cannot tell, pass here finally in brief, anonymous parade.

There are the rescuers who speak of parents. 'My mother was always concerned about everyone else.' 'I remember my mother being a person who always wanted to give from her heart.' 'My mother always reached out to others and she taught all of us to do that, too . . . I think it's in our blood.'[58] And there are the rescuers who helped save children: one who says, 'I believe in people', and who felt (at the age of forty-two), 'My life is past, but the children . . . have their life before them'; one who did what she did because 'All men are equal' and for 'no other' reason; one who 'cried when [he] went into the ghetto and . . . children clamoured after [him] . . . for help'; one who reflects that 'there are a lot of people who have no faith in human kind . . . they're only afraid for their own skin and not for yours or his or hers'; one who 'understood what it meant to be a Jew' when a six-year-old fugitive girl said what her family name had been and what it was now; and one who remembers, similarly, the anguish of the child 'who does not know why she cannot use her real name' – and who speaks as well of the preoccupation with justice and injustice that has guided her, the rescuer, all her life.[59]

Then there are those who talk about persecution: like the woman who gives as the reason for her actions that 'they [the Jews] were persecuted not because of what they did but because of the way they were born'; and the woman who says, 'he was a hunted man was all I needed to know'; and the man brought up in the belief 'that it was inadmissible to persecute people because of their race or religion'; and the man for whom the Holocaust started 'in the hearts' of people, for '[a]s soon as you go and say "That Jew!" or whatever, that's where it starts . . . As soon as you put one race higher than another one . . .'[60] This last man says also, 'if the moment's there and there's somebody in need, you go help, that's all'. He touches a pervasive theme. The rescuers speak like this: 'to give help to those who are in need'; and 'one has to help all that need it'; and 'I just had to help people who needed help and that was that. I was always ready to help the needy, always.'[61] And the rescuers speak like this: 'the worst off were the Jews. So one had to give help where people were most helpless . . .'; and 'I had to help. After all, the Jews were the most helpless people'; and 'anyone who needed help had to get it. Jews were in a specially dangerous situation . . . they had to be helped the most'; and 'My home is open to anyone in danger.'[62]

Such are the things rescuers say. They talk of their 'feeling of justice'; of learning early 'to fight for . . . justice' and early about 'helping others'; of growing up without anyone making 'a distinction between people of other religions'.[63] They say: 'There is no greater love than sacrificing your own soul for another's soul', and 'I was an old pacifist', and 'I would have helped anyone.'[64] One man says, 'I cannot stand violence.' He says, 'As a child I was taught an individual has human dignity . . .' Another man says that what he did just had to be done – 'They suffered so much'. One woman says her mother was such an unjust person that she, the daughter, developed a strong sense of justice by reaction. She says, 'I didn't help only Jews. I helped everyone who was being oppressed because of their politics or ideas.' She says, 'all my life I've been for the peaceful coexistence of all people, of all colours and religions'.[65]

It could be that these rescuers are, all of them, mistaken;

that they are really wrong about their reasons. Or it could be, on the other hand, that Richard Rorty is wrong about the Righteous.

IV

In setting out Rorty's view at the beginning of this chapter, I reported the claim he makes that it is a 'weak' explanation of a generous action to say 'because she is a human being'. It turns out that this is itself only a weak version of his claim. For in the same essay he goes on to suggest that, so far as identifying with humanity goes, in fact 'no one . . . can make *that* identification'; to him it seems an 'impossible' one.[66] Yet, the rescuers here, to say nothing of anyone else, appear to think they *can* make that identification – via notions of plain need and suffering; of human dignity and vulnerability; of equality, or justice, or a belief that we are all the children of one God. One man, indeed, finds it possible to explain himself in terms of a still wider sort of identification. This is Stefan Raczynski (the very last story to be told), whose 'father loved his fellow man' and who with the father sheltered on their farm some forty Jews, people escaping from a killing site in the nearby Polish forest. Raczynski says: 'It was a natural thing to do, like when you see a cat on the street, hungry, you give it food. When the Jews started coming from the forests and they were hungry, we gave them food . . .'[67]

Now, there is a certain irony to be noted about all this. For not only is sympathy for the need or suffering of another being – human or sometimes 'even' animal – a perfectly well-known impulse after all, and also motive or reason for action. But Rorty himself, as anyone familiar with his work will be aware, rather makes something of the fact that human beings share a common capacity for suffering. Sharing this, they are able, evidently many of them, to reach beyond fellow towns-folk and fellow bocce players. So how does it happen, then, that Rorty should deliver himself of the speculation he does about the rescuers? Let it suffice to say here that two voices contend for the ear and soul of Richard Rorty. One of these is the voice of a good, old-fashioned liberalism, of which he is an impressive and eloquent spokesman. It enjoins us to be sensitive to the susceptibility of others to pain and humiliation. It tells us, following Judith Shklar, that cruelty is the worst thing we do. But these themes push Rorty, willy-nilly, towards a notion he would shun, the notion, namely, of a *common human nature*. The second voice that calls to him cannot stand for that. It is the voice, this one, of 'anti-essentialism'; and of 'anti-foundationalism'; and also, it would seem, of anti-universalism – from which, however, the first voice, speaking of plain, never-ending human suffering, continues to beckon him away. This is a pervasive tension in Rorty's thought. I take up *its* story in the next chapter.

Referring, in another essay from *Contingency, Irony, and Solidarity*, to the work of Michael Oakeshott, Rorty commends to us the suggestion that morality be thought of 'as the voice of ourselves as members of a community, speakers of a common language'. If we see it so, he says, it will be impossible then to think 'that there is something which stands to my community as my community stands to me, some larger community called "humanity" which has an intrinsic nature.'[68] But I say: on the contrary. It is a triumph of our species, one of its most luminous achievements, to have found its way to this thought and the universalist moral principles which harmonize with it; and those like these Righteous Among the Nations who managed to live by such principles under terrifying pressure are the glory of humankind. While one should not make too much perhaps of the influence of high philosophical discussion on the wider social and political culture, one can only wonder nevertheless whether what anyone really needs right now is the effort and the energy being poured out, by philosophers, theorists of language and culture, would-be radicals, feminists, breathless messengers of the end of nearly everything, to impugn such ways of thought – as weak; impossible; or sometimes even just malign, discourse of domination and what have you.

42

V

I cannot forbear to tell here, finally, of a curious coincidence; or so at any rate it was for me. At a late stage in the work for this foregoing chapter I came upon a reference to an old article about Father Marie Benoit: yet one more rescuer, of some renown, so-called Ambassador of the Jews. This reference interested me not only because of the subject of the article but also because of its author: one James Rorty. I just had to pursue it, didn't I? James Rorty turns out to have been Richard Rorty's father.

This is what he wrote about the attitude of rescuers: 'Men and women of every class and creed, in all the occupied countries, consciously risked death and torture simply because they were revolted by the ugly cruelty of the Nazis . . . Instinctively they rejected what seemed and was a betrayal of our common humanity . . .' That seems to capture well the authentic voice of the people now called Righteous.[69]

Notes

Bibliographical details for the works of Rorty referred to here, and the abbreviations used for them, may be found at p. 147.

1. The story is from Gordon J. Horwitz, *In the Shadow of Death: Living Outside the Gates of Mauthausen*, London 1991, pp. 124–43. Regarding conditions at Mauthausen, see also Robert H. Abzug, *Inside the Vicious Heart*, New York 1985, p. 106.

2. CIS, pp. 189–91.

3. For another response to these passages in Rorty (and a good laugh), see Terry Eagleton, 'Defending the Free World', in *Socialist Register 1990*, pp. 85–6.

4. For a discussion of the issues, see Michael R. Marrus, *The Holocaust in History*, London 1989, pp. 55–107. Elsewhere Marrus and his co-author write: 'Generalizations break apart on the stubborn particularity of each of our countries.' See Michael R. Marrus and Robert O. Paxton, 'The Nazis and the Jews in Occupied Western Europe, 1940–1944', *Journal of Modern History* 54, 1982, p. 713. For comparative figures on Jewish losses, see Israel Gutman, ed., *Encyclopedia of the Holocaust* [henceforth *Encyclopedia*], London 1990, vol. 4, pp. 1797–1802.

5. Philip Friedman, *Roads to Extinction: Essays on the Holocaust*, New York 1980, pp. 411–14.

6. CIS, p. 191.

7. Philip Friedman, *Their Brothers' Keepers*, New York 1978, pp. 30–32.

8. See, for example, EHO, p. 1; Ths, pp. 564, 572, 578 n. 23; and Fem, pp. 5, 12 n. 18.

9. Andre Stein, *Quiet Heroes: True Stories of the Rescue of Jews by Christians in Nazi-Occupied Holland* [henceforth Stein], Toronto 1988, p. 93.

10. Louis de Jong, 'Help to People in Hiding', in Michael R. Marrus, ed., *The Nazi Holocaust 5: Public Opinion and Relations to the Jews in Nazi Europe*, Westport (Conn.) 1989, vol. 2, p. 639. Regarding the burdens on women, see: Stein, pp. 7, 47, 188, 191–4; Samuel P. Oliner and Pearl M. Oliner, *The Altruistic Personality: Rescuers of Jews in Nazi Europe* [henceforth AP], New York 1992, pp. 83–4; and Gay Block and Malka Drucker, *Rescuers. Portraits of Moral Courage in the Holocaust* [henceforth Block], New York 1992, pp. 63, 82.

11. For some accounts of such cases, see Nechama Tec, *When Light Pierced the Darkness* [henceforth Tec], Oxford 1986, pp. 63–8.

12. See Moshe Bejski, 'The "Righteous among the Nations" and their Part in the Rescue of Jews' [henceforth Bejski], in Marrus, *The Nazi Holocaust 5*, vol. 2, pp. 452–3; and *Encyclopedia*, vol. 3, pp. 1280–81.

13. Block, p. 252.

14. Yehuda Bauer, *The Holocaust in Historical Perspective*, Seattle 1978, p. 77; Bejski, p. 461.

15. Tec, pp. 115–19, 127–8; Oliners, AP, pp. 127–9. See also the results of a study by Manfred Wolfson reported in Lawrence Baron, 'The Holocaust and Human Decency: A Review of Research on the Rescue of Jews in Nazi Occupied Europe' [henceforth Baron], *Humboldt Journal of Social Relations* 13, 1985/86, pp. 239–40.

16. Friedman, *Roads to Extinction*, p. 414; Pierre Sauvage, in Carol Rittner and Sondra Myers, eds., *The Courage to Care: Rescuers of Jews During the Holocaust* [henceforth Rittner], New York 1986, p. 137; Sarah Gordon, *Hitler, Germans, and the "Jewish Question"*, Princeton 1984, pp. 218–21; and Baron, pp. 239–40.

17. Bauer, *The Holocaust in Historical Perspective*, p. 76; Tec, pp. 127–8; Oliners, AP, pp. 159–60; and Baron, pp. 239–40.

18. Tec, pp. 137–9, 145–9; Oliners, AP, pp. 155–7; Baron, pp. 239– 40; P. M. Oliner and S. P. Oliner, 'Rescuers of Jews During the Holocaust' [henceforth RJ], in Yehuda Bauer, *Remembering for the Future* [henceforth RFTF], Oxford 1989, vol. I, pp. 510–13; Mordecai Paldiel, 'The Altruism of the Righteous Gentiles' [henceforth Paldiel], RFTF, vol. I, p. 520.

19. Cf. the remarks of Paldiel, pp. 520–21.

20. Perry London, 'The Rescuers: Motivational Hypotheses about Christians Who Saved Jews from the Nazis', in J. Macaulay and L. Berkowitz, eds., *Altruism and Helping Behaviour*, New York 1970, pp. 241-50.

21. Douglas Huneke, 'Glimpses of Light in a Vast Darkness', RFTF, vol. I, pp. 489-90, and 'A Study of Christians Who Rescued Jews During the Nazi Era', *Humboldt Journal of Social Relations* 9, 1981/82, p. 146 [henceforth, respectively, GL and SC]; Samuel P. Oliner, 'The Need to Recognize the Heroes of the Nazi Era', in Marrus, *The Nazi Holocaust 5*, vol. 2, p. 482, and 'The Unsung Heroes in Nazi Occupied Europe', *Nationalities Papers* 12, 1984, p. 135 [henceforth NR and UH]; and Tec, pp. 152, 154.

22. Huneke, GL, p. 489, and SC, p. 146; Oliner, UH, p. 135, and NR, p. 479. And cf. Oliners, AP, p. 142, and RJ, p. 509.

23. Baron, pp. 243-4; Oliners, AP, p. 176.

24. Tec, p. 181; Paldiel, p. 520.

25. Huneke, GL, p. 491, and SC, p. 146.

26. Oliner, NR, pp. 480, 482, and UH, pp. 134-5; Baron, pp. 245, 239-40.

27. Tec, pp. 129 (and 227), 178 (and 233); Oliners, AP, p. 81.

28. Oliners, AP, p. 115; Tec, p. 227.

29. Tec, p. 178.

30. Bejski, pp. 460-61; Stein, p. 310; Eva Fleischner, 'Can the Few Become the Many? Some Catholics in France Who Saved Jews During the Holocaust' [henceforth Fleischner], RFTF, I, pp. 241, 243; Kristen R. Monroe, 'Altruism and the Theory of Rational Action: Rescuers of Jews in Nazi Europe' [henceforth Monroe], *Ethics* 101, 1990, pp. 117-18, 122; Huneke, SC, pp. 146-7, and GL, p. 491.

31. Oliner, UH, pp. 134-5, and NR, p. 482; Oliners, RJ, pp. 507-9, and AP, pp. 163-70, 287; Tec, pp. 132, 145, 154; Paldiel, pp. 522-3.

32. Cf. CoP, pp. xxix-xxx.

33. Though rescuers are mostly identified by their real names, in some of the sources I draw upon they are given fictitious ones to preserve confidentiality. As the sources themselves make it clear which practice is being followed, I simply use the names given, real or fictitious as the case may be.

34. Their story, like many here, is told in the wonderful book of Gay Block and Malka Drucker, *Rescuers*, pp. 62-7. For Douwes, see also *Encyclopedia*, vol. 1, pp. 401-2.

35. Block, pp. 52, 57; Rittner, pp. 59, 65.

36. Tec, pp. 134-5, 139-40, 177-8; Rittner, p. 89; Bejski, pp. 468-70. For Duckwitz, see also *Encyclopedia*, vol. 1, p. 409.

37. Stein, pp. 18-20, 32; and pp. 183-5, 187, 191.

38. Rittner, p. 43; Block, pp. 232, 226. For Graebe, see also *Encyclopedia*, vol. 2, pp. 599-600, and Martin Gilbert, *The Holocaust: The Jewish Tragedy*, London 1987, pp. 476-8.

39. Fleischner, pp. 234–7; Friedman, *Their Brothers' Keepers*, pp. 49–50.
40. Block, pp. 128–31.
41. Block, pp. 68–71; Stein, pp. 58–9.
42. Tec, pp. 107–8, 111–12.
43. Tec, pp. 101–6, 175.
44. Block, pp. 42–6; Monroe, pp. 107, 118.
45. Block, pp. 84–9.
46. Block, pp. 163–5.
47. Tec, pp. 133–4, 160–61, 177.
48. Block, pp. 237–40; Tec, pp. 145, 165 (original punctuation).
49. Block, pp. 192–6; Rittner, pp. 44–51; Monroe, pp. 107, 119.
50. Tec, pp. 70–71, 165–6; Stein, pp. 222–4, 245; Block, pp. 136–41; 208–11; and 94–7.
51. Oliners, AP, pp. 193–9; Block, pp. 58–61, and Stein, pp. 102, 134. Steenstra's story is given under a fictitious name in Stein. I have felt free to use her real name here because it is given in Block, presumably with her agreement.
52. Block, pp. 220–23; pp. 241–5.
53. Block, pp. 180–85.
54. Oliners, AP, pp. 203–4.
55. Block, pp. 78–83; Rittner, pp. 24–7; Oliners, AP, pp. 215–20, 228. See my remarks at note 51 above. They apply here too, to Johtje Vos.
56. Block, pp. 33–41; Rittner, pp. 28–33.
57. Oliners, AP, pp. 142–4; Stein, pp. 141, 144, 166; Block, pp. 149–52.
58. Block, pp. 166, 176, 215.
59. Block, pp. 204–7; Oliners, AP, p. 213; Block, pp. 188, 26, 48, 102–5.
60. Block, p. 77; Fleischner, p. 239; Block, pp. 114, 27.
61. Block, p. 32; Rittner, p. 107; Tec, pp. 170, 167.
62. Tec, pp. 176, 177; Stein, p. 266.
63. Block, pp. 124, 118, 142.
64. Block, pp. 249, 146; Tec, p. 176.
65. Block, p. 172; Fleischner, p. 238; Block, pp. 153–7.
66. CIS, p. 198; emphases in the original.
67. Block, pp. 197–201.
68. CIS, p. 59. Compare the words of Maria Langthaler quoted at the beginning of this chapter.
69. James Rorty, 'Father Benoit: "Ambassador of the Jews". An Untold Chapter of the Underground', *Commentary* 2, December 1946, pp. 507–13, at p. 513. On James Rorty, see Alan M. Wald, *The New York Intellectuals*, Chapel Hill, N.C., and London 1987, pp. 54–5 and *passim*.

'That Most Complex Being'

The centrality of arguments about human nature to social and political theories is a familiar theme to students of the subject. Such arguments may be of an affirmative kind, asserting some given characteristic or behaviour pattern as generally or typically human. Nearly as often perhaps they will be self-consciously negative, denying there is anything of substance to be brought usefully under the heading of 'human nature'. In addition to explicit assertion and counter-assertion of this kind, there are usually also, informing any theoretically elaborated view about politics or society, some less overt, less considered assumptions in the matter.

One philosopher who expresses himself emphatically about human nature, and whose works have attracted wide interest, is Richard Rorty. Rorty is, on the face of it, attached to the second of the two generic standpoints just described: he denies any intrinsic or universal human nature. The denial is part of a broader commitment, to what he commends at one point as 'a generalized anti-essentialism'.[1] But that is on the face of it. Closer analysis reveals a more complicated picture. In what follows I explore Rorty's various usages on the question of human nature and the tensions and anomalies as I shall argue they display.

Rorty is an astute and provocative as well as influential thinker. Detailed attention to his work may need no greater justification than that. All the same, the sort of conceptions to be explored here are of a more general interest. They are to be found not only, as they have long been, amongst political radicals of one kind and another, but are popular also with the enthusiasts of post-modernism. These are currently many. Though Rorty's own relationship to post-modernism is not an altogether enthusiastic one,[2] the aforesaid anti-essentialism is a trope he has in common with it. An analysis of what he says about the idea of human nature, then, may serve a wider effort of clarification and exchange.

After some preliminary remarks, I examine six recurrent types of usage on this issue in Rorty's work. I go on to offer a few reflections on the story they conjointly tell.

I

One or more of a number of things can be involved in arguments about human nature. Three such things are these:

(1) claims about characteristics held to be shared by human beings cross-culturally and transhistorically;

(2) attempts to focus on some putative *differentia specifica*, on a shared characteristic or set of characteristics that distinguishes humankind from other species;

(3) the identification of traits thought to be of normative importance, guiding us towards better ways to live or constraining how we should treat one another.

(3) is often linked to (2) and/or (1) – judgements of normative importance to qualities held to be universal, whether humanly specific or not – via notions of potentiality and limitation.

It will be my contention here that in each of three meanings indicated by these three sorts of concern Rorty clearly relies on a conception of human nature. And yet his books are replete with dismissals of the idea. How does this come about? It comes about, I shall argue, in two ways. The first is by a kind of continual shifting of ground, so that in now one, now another meaning, a human nature is denied by Rorty, even while in one or other of the meanings not currently being denied a human nature is also implicitly affirmed by him. J. L. Austin, as Rorty himself tells us, once put this so: 'There's the bit where you say it and the bit where you take it back.'[3] The second way is through a tendency on Rorty's part to suggest that in order to subscribe to a notion of human nature you must be committed to something so excessively narrow and specific as to have to overlook differences, historical, cultural or simply inter-individual, that are manifest and impossible to deny.

I shall support these claims by reviewing the major critical uses and rhetorical emphases of Rorty's omnipresent rejection of the idea of a human nature. Each of the five sub-sections to follow carries a brief opening paraphrase of the Rortian theme it documents and discusses.

(a) *There is nothing to people other than what is the result of their socialization (such as the capacity to communicate with one another through language).*

Rorty sometimes writes as though people were simply what their society and culture make of them. They have no inherent nature. We may begin by noting the relation of this discursive figure to the broader anti-essentialist viewpoint of which it is a part. What is needed, according to Rorty, is 'a repudiation of the very idea of anything – mind or matter, self or world – having an intrinsic nature to be expressed or represented.' Such an idea, 'that the world or the self has an intrinsic nature . . . is a remnant of the idea that the world is a divine creation.'[4] 'The absence of an intrinsic human nature',[5] then, belongs for him to a more general existential situation.

We are not to think, in any case, that '"the human sciences" have a nature, any more than we think that man does'; or that 'there is something which stands to my community as my community stands to me, some larger community called "humanity" which has an intrinsic nature';

or that '"humanity" ha[s] a nature over and above the various forms of life which history has thrown up so far.'[6] Rorty suggests that Foucault did not perhaps accept without all reservation 'that the self, the human subject, is simply whatever acculturation makes of it'. Putting the same point otherwise, he says that 'Socialization . . . goes all the way down.'[7]

If there is nothing intrinsic in human beings, are there any universal traits? It does not follow as a matter of strict entailment that there could not be, since by a large transhistorical accident globally common and continuous forms of socialization might have occurred – although the probability of that may seem low. Rorty appears to reject the notion of any such universal. The job of the novelist, he says, 'can only be undertaken with a whole heart by someone untroubled by dreams of an ahistorical framework within which human history is enacted, a universal human nature by reference to which history can be explained . . .' He speaks, similarly, of a need to 'avoid the embarrassments of the universalist claim that the term "human being" . . . names an unchanging essence, an ahistorical natural kind with a permanent set of intrinsic features.'[8]

It may seem, therefore, that Rorty rejects the idea of a human nature in the first of the three meanings flagged above. According to this – (1) – our human nature would be just those characteristics which are an intrinsic part of our make-up and as such universally shared. But in *this* meaning Rorty does not in fact reject the idea of a human nature, however things may seem. By principles of ordinary interpretative charity we can take every appearance of such a rejection as being merely an incomplete statement of his view. For there are places where he makes plain the awareness of something that is inherent and common to all human beings.

(b) *The only thing we share with other human beings we also share with other animals: susceptibility to pain.*

Rorty here and there puts a qualifier on his denial of intrinsic and universal traits. It is not that there are no such traits at all, only that there are none that are distinctively human. Rorty is with the 'historicist thinkers . . . [who] have denied that there is such a thing as "human nature" . . . [who] insist that socialization, and thus historical circumstance, goes all the way down – that there is nothing "beneath" socialization or prior to history which is definatory of the human.' Or again, he is with those who 'have given up the Enlightenment assumption that religion, myth, and tradition can be opposed to something ahistorical, something common to all human beings qua human'.[9] The inherent qualities people have in common they also have in common with other species: 'the only intrinsic features of human beings are those they share with the brutes – for example, the ability to suffer and inflict pain.'[10]

Now, one might think it a pedantic quibble to suggest, in light of this specification, that some amendment of the usages exemplified in (a) above would be appropriate. For, in the light of it, people are then more than simply what socialization or acculturation makes of them; permanent features, hence some kinds of universalist claim, should not be so embarrassing; and so on. In some ways, perhaps this is a quibble. But two questions are to the point nevertheless. First, is there any good reason for the regular use of discursive forms that tend to obscure the existence of characteristics human beings do indeed have in common – albeit that these are not distinctively human characteristics? Granted, no novelist will get very far with her eyes fixed only on them. Should they be held on that account as unimportant from every point of view? Rorty, as we shall see, does not think so. Second, even if what is thus common to human beings is not a specifically *human* nature – because like pain, it 'is what we human beings have that ties us to the nonlanguage-using beasts'[11] – why is it not still a nature, the sort of intrinsic entity repudiated by Rorty for 'anything'? And how would the idea of *this* sort of intrinsic entity willy-nilly implicate the person entertaining it in a belief in divine creation?[12] In other words, even if, on an adjusted definition, the denial of a human nature still stands, 'generalized anti-essentialism' would already seem to be more precarious.

I shall return to the issue raised by the first of these questions, regarding the importance of intrinsic features like the ability to suffer pain, in section II below. The questions about anti-essentialism are the subject of Chapter 4. I now formalize the situation reached so far with the hypothesis that it might then be rather in the second of the three meanings flagged earlier that Rorty dismisses the idea of a human nature. According to this meaning – (2) – our human nature would be those common traits people share that are, in addition, distinctively human. In the usages illustrated here at (b), Rorty suggests there are no such traits. But this way of understanding his repudiation of human nature is equally problematic. For he also affirms categorically that there are some such traits.

(c) *Human beings, however they have been socialized, do share a susceptibility other animals lack: to a particular sort of pain. They can be humiliated by the violent disruption of their patterns of belief and cherished values.*

Rorty knows as well as anyone that we have species-specific qualities. Amongst them is 'that special sort of pain which the brutes do not share with the humans – humiliation.' We have 'a common susceptibility to humiliation'.[13] We are vulnerable to it by virtue of the beliefs and attachments that can be belittled and exposed to ridicule; and because a person can be coerced into doing or saying and sometimes even thinking things 'which later she will be unable to cope with having done or thought.'[14] As Rorty also says, '. . . the best way to cause people long-lasting pain is to humiliate them by making the things that seemed most important to them look futile, obsolete, and powerless.'[15]

It will be readily evident that, involving as it does our structures of value and belief, this capacity we have and other animals lack, to be subjected to a particular kind of pain, is predicated on further capacities that we have and they lack. One is the capacity for language; another the more general capacity it yields for symbolic inventiveness and individuality. Rorty refers to the human specificity of these capacities. He speaks, for instance, of 'the sort of pain which the torturer hopes to create in his victim by depriving him of language and thereby of a connection with human institutions'. He writes with regard to Freud: 'By seeing every human being as consciously or unconsciously acting out an idiosyncratic fantasy, we can see the distinctively human, as opposed to animal, portion of each human life as the use for symbolic purposes of every particular person, object, situation, event, and word encountered in later life.' He quotes with approval Lionel Trilling's view of Freud – who 'showed us that poetry is indigenous to the very constitution of the mind'.[16]

A question arising now is whether and how history can be explained *without* reference to such human abilities as these.[17] But the question I shall instead pursue is why Rorty should sometimes, as we have seen at (b) above, deny that people share a common nature composed of characteristics specific to them as humans, when he also affirms precisely such common human characteristics. One suggestion, which I consider briefly only to set aside, might be this. Though there are some humanly specific traits, they are not a nature because they are not intrinsic. We only acquire them by being socialized. Well, in a way they are not intrinsic, but in a way they also are. Language and the rest does not come 'naturally' to an altogether isolated human being. But that it comes only to a human being when not isolated, when socialized, is a consequence of capacities that are intrinsic to that being. Another way of putting this is to say that it is not because they have not been socialized, or socialized properly, that animals do not read Heidegger.

These are banal points. Rorty knows and uses the concept of 'human potentiality'.[18] And he is as emphatic about its natural basis as it is possible to be without calling it a natural basis. 'Language', he has told an interviewer, '. . . [is] an ability which distinguishes us from other intelligent animals and enables us to perform actions which are not accessible to them . . . [P]ragmatism considers language as the ability to attain higher purposes, outside the scope of and even inconceivable for the animals, who are deprived of it.'[19]

Let us therefore consider another suggestion. If Rorty relies on a notion of human nature on the second as well as on the first of the three meanings I have distinguished, but just not under the heading 'human nature', perhaps the reason for his denials really lies elsewhere than it so often appears to lie: with some concern other than what traits there are common to human beings, or what traits there are both common to and distinctive of them.

(d) *There is nothing within all of us, no common human nature, no inherent fellow feeling or unity of interest, to use as a moral reference point.*

Rorty often writes in this vein: 'Habermas and Derrida . . . disagree about whether there is something universally human to serve as a foundation for ethics'; and he is with Derrida in finding Habermas's sort of universalism 'pointlessly "metaphysical"'.[20] He (Rorty) is one of those 'people who say that "humanity" is a biological rather than a moral notion'. Again: 'The absence of an intrinsic human nature, and thus of built-in moral obligations, seems to us pragmatists compatible with any and every decision about what sort of life to lead, or what sort of politics to pursue.'[21]

Rorty proposes that we might think of ourselves as being machines, artefacts: 'If humanity is a natural kind, then perhaps we can find our centre and so learn how to live well. But if we are machines, then it is up to us to invent a use for ourselves.' And if we are machines, we can see ourselves as requiring 'much tinkering, rather than as a substance with a precious essence to be discovered and cherished'.[22] To put the point in another way again, we can 'erase the picture of the self common to Greek metaphysics, Christian theology and Enlightenment rationalism: the picture of an ahistorical natural centre, the locus of human dignity, surrounded by an adventitious and inessential periphery'.[23]

The suggestion one can accordingly now consider is that what Rorty actually repudiates is the idea of a human nature in the third of the meanings earlier signalled. On this meaning – (3) – a human nature would be a set of characteristics common to human beings that provided also a moral reference point: for shaping or constraining our thinking about human dignity, how to live well, our moral obligations, and so on.

The suggestion is supported by one other feature of his work, namely a distaste for the language of emancipation. That is, once again, a typically 'post-modern' stance. Rorty is opposed to the 'conviction that there is an interesting general theory about human beings or their oppression'; refers to 'the disappearance of the transcendental subject – of "man" as something having a nature which society can repress or understand'.[24] By the same token, utopia for him, a good society, is not what it is on account of being in harmony with some such putative nature. We would be wrong, Rorty says, to think of a 'common humanity' as the philosophical foundation for democratic politics. Followers of Dewey like himself 'would like to praise parliamentary democracy and the welfare state as very good things, but only on the basis of invidious comparisons with suggested concrete alternatives, not on the basis of claims that these institutions are truer to human nature . . .'.[25] The 'pragmatist utopia is . . . not one in which human nature has been unshackled', and pragmatists do not want 'narratives of emancipation'.[26] What they favour is cultural pluralism, as being apt to the spirit of tolerance in democratic politics – a spirit 'neutral on questions of what is central to human life, questions about the goal or point of human existence'.[27]

So, there is a lot in Rorty to support the suggestion that a major concern of his in disparaging the idea of a human nature is its normative usage. There may be readers who will find this suggestion problematic nevertheless, in view of some of what has already passed before us. Focusing, for example, on Rorty's denial of an ahistorical centre as the locus of human *dignity*, they might wonder then about the common human susceptibility to *humiliation*; or equally about the ability he says language gives us to attain purposes that are *higher*. Both humiliation and higher purposes can be related in familiar ways to notions of human dignity. There could, though, be a persuasive response to this sort of doubt. Rorty perhaps intended 'higher', in that usage of it, in some purely technical sense, and means 'humiliation', likewise, as a descriptive concept only (the kind of pain people feel in such and such circumstances etc.), and consequently is not involved by either term in the sort of moral evaluation which, on the other hand, he maybe does reckon 'human dignity' to carry. Thus there is nothing here to show that, rejecting the idea of a human nature as moral reference point, Rorty himself also relies on the idea of a human nature as moral reference point. All the same, he does rely on it as that.

(e) *The worst thing you can do to someone, beyond causing them acute pain, is to use that pain so that they will be unable to reconstitute themselves when it is over.*

According to Rorty, 'cruelty is the worst thing we do.' This is a central, repeated point with him and he follows Judith Shklar in making it definitive of liberal belief.[28]

Cruelty *is* the worst thing we do. But cruelty is deliberately inflicting suffering; it is delight in, or indifference to, the pain of others. Rorty knows these obvious connections. One way for him of being 'very cruel' is to cause that special sort of pain which is humiliating people.[29]

The normative priority of this concern of his is something about which Rorty is himself emphatic. He discourages his readers 'from slipping into a political attitude which will lead you to think that there is some social goal more important than avoiding cruelty'.[30] And he warns, correspondingly, against the figure of the 'ascetic priest' – whose goal is 'the ineffable', and a bit of whom there is in every philosopher. Ascetic priests are impatient with 'mere happiness or mere decrease of suffering'; or with 'the mere pursuit of pleasure and avoidance of pain'.[31] Rorty proffers to them the rejoinder (as he says this is) of the novelist: 'It is comical to think that *anyone* could transcend the quest for happiness, to think that any theory could be more than a means to happiness, that there is something called Truth which transcends pleasure and pain.' As a liberal is someone who thinks cruelty the worst thing we do, so a democratic utopia would be one in which 'nobody would dream of thinking that there is something realer than pleasure or pain.'[32]

Ability to suffer pain, remember, is one of the intrinsic features human beings share with the brutes; and the special pain of humiliation is a common susceptibilty we share with other human beings, however socialized, although not with the brutes. The worst thing we do, therefore, Rorty characterizes by reference to a human nature in both of meanings (1) and (2). But as it is precisely the *worst* thing we do, the idea of a human nature serves him as a moral reference point – that is, in meaning (3) as well, and his disclaimers with respect to this meaning in turn notwithstanding.

Rorty's reliance upon what he also simultaneously disclaims finds some concentrated forms of expression in his pages. Here is one example:

> A society which took its moral vocabulary from novels . . . would not ask itself questions about human nature, the point of human existence, or the meaning of human life. Rather, it would ask itself what we can do so as to get along with each other, how we can arrange things so as to be comfortable with one another, how institutions can be changed so that everyone's right to be understood has a better chance of being gratified.[33]

There is, doubtless, good enough reason for withholding the descriptions, 'the point of human existence' and 'the meaning of human life', from the purposes of getting along and being comfortable with one another. Where some have thought the glorification of God, the flourishing of high culture, self-actualization and what have you to be that point or meaning, Rorty says we should just do what we can to get along together without bothering to think of this in such terms.

Is there really no question here at all, though, 'about human nature'? His own favoured goal, it is true, is one that is more open, less specific, than are alternatives of this ilk. But it is not so obviously so in relation to every such alternative, as 'self-actualization' in the foregoing list may remind us. Perhaps the important difference is supposed to be that where these other purposes have been consciously grounded by their sponsors on an idea of human nature – grounded, as upon a foundation – Rorty for his part offers his benign goal as ungrounded; merely free-floating advice. Except that we already know what for him defines some of the parameters of getting along and being comfortable with one another. Everyone's 'right to be understood', for example, is clearly related to the goal of sparing people that specially human pain of being humiliated.

Here is a second example of the same kind of concentrated tension:

> The view I am offering says that there is such a thing as moral progress, and that this progress is indeed in the direction of greater human solidarity. But that solidarity is not thought of as recognition of a core self, the human essence, in all human beings. Rather, it is thought of as the ability to see more and more traditional differences (of tribe, religion, race, customs, and the like) as unimportant when compared with similarities with respect to pain and humiliation.[34]

This seems to me again to reintroduce the character it has just ejected, presenting her merely in different shoes. Solidarity may well not merit being designated part of a core self or human essence. Still, there they are, those similarities with respect to pain and humiliation, compared with which so much diversity for Rorty is unimportant – unimportant from a moral point of view.

A third and last example takes us back to the issue of emancipation:

> There is no human nature which was once, or still is, in chains. Rather, our species has – ever since it developed language – been making up a nature for itself . . . Lately our species has been making up a particularly good nature for itself – that produced by the institutions of the liberal West. When we praise this development, we pragmatists drop the revolutionary rhetoric of emancipation and unmasking in favour of a reformist rhetoric about increased tolerance and decreased suffering.[35]

From one angle, this is the familiar discourse of historicist denial of human nature: there is no such thing as human nature, it is said, because we form and transform ourselves, or are formed by our social relations; we make up our own nature. In fact, we do and we also don't, as is borne out by, amongst other things, the important similarities with respect to pain and humiliation.

My concern now, however, is not so much with the existence of these similarities as with their simultaneous renunciation and use by Rorty as a moral reference point. In this regard, dropping the rhetoric of emancipation changes nothing. 'Human nature unshackled' or 'in chains' does have a somewhat archaic ring, of which the talk of 'increased tolerance and decreased suffering' is free. But where the former has explicit recourse to an underlying human constitution as moral reference point, the latter has implicit recourse to it, that is all. It has implicit recourse to it via a notion of the ills human beings will generally want to avoid; whether in virtue of being, like other animals, susceptible to pain; or of being, unlike them, attached to beliefs, values, identities and so on, which are crucial to their well-being, so making them vulnerable to further awful, humanly specific kinds of hurt. It is this vulnerability that makes the value of tolerance appropriate in human affairs. The less, as much as the more, archaic rhetoric, therefore, aims at or hopes for a set of social and political arrangements that can be said, perfectly meaningfully, to be in greater conformity with some intrinsic and shared human characteristics. And since it comes to this, what then is actually wrong with the rhetoric of emancipation? But I leave that question and return to it later.

Let us pause here. Before going further, I want to review the path we have travelled so far. I shall do so by offering a short quotation from Rorty to represent each of the previous subsections (a) to (e).

(a) 'There is nothing to people except what has been socialized into them – their ability to use language, and thereby to exchange beliefs and desires with other people.'

(b) '. . . all we share with all other humans is the same thing we share with all other animals – the ability to feel pain.'

(c) '. . . human beings who have been socialized – socialized in any language, any culture – do share a capacity which other animals lack. They can all be given a special kind of pain: They can all be humiliated by the forcible tearing down of the particular structures of language and belief in which they were socialized (or which they pride themselves on having formed for themselves).'

(d) '. . . there is nothing deep inside each of us, no common human nature, no built-in human solidarity, to use as a moral reference point.'

(e) '. . . the worst thing you can do to somebody is not to make her scream in agony but to use that agony in such a way that even when the agony is over, she cannot reconstitute herself.'

Each of these passages raises a question about the content of one or more of its neighbours. Readers may now like to confirm for themselves that the headline summaries with which I began the five sub-sections (a) to (e) above were based, loosely, on these passages: (a) there on (a) here, and so forth for (b) through (e). They will be able to confirm for themselves also that these five passages all come from the same place. They all come from page 177 of *Contingency, Irony, and Solidarity*.

As displayed here, of course, the passages are not embedded in their native context. This is a recontextualization of them. But I do not believe that, using them so, I have misrepresented the several meanings and – as I have sought to bring out – logical tensions present in Rorty's thinking on this issue. On the contrary, the procedure I have followed has attempted to document the wide extent of their presence there. The only more particular interest of these five passages is the fact that they all come from the one page. Can further light be thrown on this strange (or so I perceive it, anyway) state of affairs? Perhaps some can, if we now look at one other kind of usage. It, too, can be exemplified from the same page.

(f) 'To be a person is to speak a *particular* language, one which enables us to discuss particular beliefs and desires with particular sorts of people.'

A recurrent suggestion in Rorty's work is that to believe in a common human nature you must be, not just aware of some human universals, but blinded by them. Thus, you must think of human nature as 'an inner structure which leads all members of the species to converge to the same point, to recognize the same theories, virtues, and works of art as worthy of honour'. You must dream 'of an ultimate community which will have transcended the distinction between the natural and the social'.[36] And you must refuse individual diversity. Rorty writes of Freud that he enabled us to understand 'both

61

Nietzsche's superman and Kant's common moral consciousness' as alternative forms or strategies of life:

> There is much to be said for both. Each has advantages and dis-
> advantages. Decent people are often rather dull. Great wits are
> sure to madness near allied. Freud stands in awe before the poet,
> but describes him as infantile. He is bored by the merely moral
> man, but describes him as mature . . . He does not see a need to
> erect a theory of human nature which will safeguard the interests
> of the one or the other. He sees . . . neither as 'more truly human'
> than the other.[37]

What can one say? Indeed, there are conceptions of human
nature so narrow as to obscure or repress real differences,
societal and individual, to flatten out the enormous variety of
human motivation and potentiality. To get off the starting
block, a persuasive conception of human nature must clearly
be able to accommodate particularity: the moral person and
the poet, divergent patterns of belief and value, different languages. Still, a particular language, to take only this, is a
language; it is dependent as such on 'an ability which distinguishes us from other intelligent animals';[38] and language is
crucial, on Rorty's own account of things, to every human
enterprise, moral, poetic or whatever.

Nor need referring particular languages to the general
human capacity they depend on tie one to a hopeless notion of
one day 'transcending' the distinction between the natural
and the social. On the contrary, so referring them is just a
reminder that there is that distinction, irreducibly – as there
would not be if socialization really did go all the way down.
In saying (when he does say it) that the sole intrinsic traits are
ones we share with animals, like 'the ability to suffer and
inflict pain', Rorty qualifies 'intrinsic' to mean 'untouched by
historical change'.[39] But why should anyone understand it
so: as indicating some pristine, altogether umodified nature?
The most elementary bodily needs – to eat, to excrete, for
rest – are in an important sense not untouched by historical

change. Nor even is the ability to inflict pain, however it may be with the ability to suffer it. But such needs and abilities are also not *wholly* determined by the historical change that touches them. To deny that they constitute an inherent nature is merely to dissolve one kind of reality in favour of another. There is no nature here, supposedly, because there is a history. One could with equal validity say – the very sort of thing Rorty is so concerned to have us abjure – that there is no history here because it is all down to a (human) nature. Or on the other hand: one can abjure both ways of speaking, in favour of maintaining an indispensable distinction.

Rorty's rhetorical strategy in this, the affirmation of particularity and historical change as telling against any common human nature, is standard in historicist argument on the topic. The strategy is to insist that the concept of human nature must carry more weight than it plausibly can carry and then to reject it because it cannot. With respect again to solidarity, for instance, Rorty proffers the contrasting standpoints of two characters he dubs, not entirely neutrally, the liberal ironist and the liberal metaphysician – the latter wanting reference to a human nature, whilst the former eschews it. The metaphysician, we are told, wants our wish to be kind 'to be bolstered by an argument . . . which will highlight a common human essence, an essence which is something more than our shared ability to suffer humiliation'. The ironist for her part just makes do with pain and humiliation.[40] Now, perhaps some people do want something more than this. But they need not want it. In the context of the present discussion, it is quite enough. To add, as Rorty does here, that the ironist's feeling of solidarity 'is based on a sense of a common danger, not on a common possession or a shared power' is only camouflage. Call it, at this point, a danger and not a power or possession; but it is in any case common to us as humans, part of a make-up or constitution we share, which is just what many understand by a human nature; and the thing is also called by Rorty a susceptibility, an ability and a capacity, all of them, these, a little bit like a power.

They are not the sort of power, however, that Rorty has in mind upon the moment, and this is the real business now. For, the something more you must want of human beings for there to be a common human nature, is 'their relation to a larger shared power – rationality, God, truth, or history, for example'. I pass over rationality: one name, currently much maligned, for an important human capacity. But the presence of the Deity in this list, and of truth and history as hypostatized, free-standing – 'larger' – powers, yields the secret. Belief in a human nature is *ipso facto* belief in some telos or destiny. It is belief in a goal that is precisely metaphysical, one lodged perhaps at the end of an inexorable history. Here is Rorty insisting on the openness of the future:

> I take Orwell to be telling us that whether our future rulers are more like O'Brien or more like J. S. Mill does not depend . . . on deep facts about human nature. For, as O'Brien and Humbert Humbert show, intellectual gifts – intelligence, judgement, curiosity, imagination, a taste for beauty – are as malleable as the sexual instinct. They are as capable of as many diverse employments as the human hand . . . What our future rulers will be like will not be determined by any large necessary truths about human nature and its relation to truth and justice, but by a lot of small contingent facts.[41]

Contingent ones, yes; though one may wonder why they may not be both large and small, comprising structural causes and trends as well as little accidents. But in any event if those rulers turn out to be more like O'Brien, things will go worse for human beings – on account of some facts and truths, whether deep or not, about their nature. And although a metaphysical teleology may sometimes be a conception of human nature, this is like Valéry being a petty-bourgeois intellectual. Not every conception of human nature is a metaphysical teleology.

II

I offer now a few concluding observations. The first of them anticipates this question: do we not have though, it might be asked, in the sort of matter just surveyed under (f), a resolution of any outstanding problem or puzzle concerning Rorty's anti-human nature discourse? The resolution would be that what he really means in dismissing the idea of a human nature is not what I mean in defending it. He means rather a conception in which – (4) – to affirm a human nature is to overlook or seriously understate cultural and individual diversity and/or to believe in some telos or destiny, a pre-given point of human existence. As it is not sensible thus variously to overlook, understate and believe, Rorty has sound reason for denying a human nature in his preferred sense, even while others like me continue to affirm one in our preferred sense. Everything is then level, surely.

No. For, while it is indeed the case that Rorty does mean something like (4), it is not all he means. Or at any rate it is not all he says. He also avails himself freely of rhetorical conveniences not pertinent to that meaning: telling us that there are no intrinsic or permanent features of human beings; that the self is simply what acculturation makes of it; that all we share as humans we also share with other species; that there is nothing universal or common to us to use as a basis of ethical judgement, nothing to repress or understand; and so on. What is all this for? One could after all just say, for example, 'there is no human nature in the sense of a metaphysical purpose or destiny implanted in each human being' – and leave it at that.

What we have with (4) is not Rorty's 'real' or only meaning but a meaning, so to say, of last resort. It is the inner, defensible core of a fighting position with a number of outlying rhetorical fortifications, all of which are visibly fragile and in one way or another soon abandoned by the people behind them. Thus is it always, with the radical, the comprehensive, denial of a human nature. The defensible core turns out to be less interesting than the outer wall. That there is nothing at all common to human beings or inherent in their make-up is at least startling when you think about it. But that there is no human nature *just* in the sense of there being no inner link of the human individual to an immanent theological or meta-historical purpose (or to a preordained order of lordship and servitude, capitalist forms of ownership, purely procreative sexuality, benevolent or malign intent, etc.); *even though* some common characteristics are to be allowed when all is said and done – this can also be rendered by saying that there is only the sort of human nature there is, and not the sort that there isn't. It is a less than arresting proposition.

Second, I anticipate also, now, the objection that Rorty's core position can be taken separately from whatever he may say inconsistently with it. Isolating this position analytically from anything that so obscures it, we will do better to stay with it as a conception of human nature than to go with the sort of notion I am here defending. This is because such common traits of human beings as there actually are do not add up to anything substantial enough to constitute a useful notion.

A short response to this is that definition is free. You can stay or go with what you want. You can define 'human nature' in so narrow a way that there will not be one. You may then want a word for what there nonetheless is in that domain. A longer response is that the judgement as to what does and does not count as substantial or useful can, however, also be put under scrutiny. By what criterion or in what context, bearing on the understanding of the ways of human beings, is a notion of their nature according to which they are susceptible to pain and humiliation, have the capacity for language and (in a large sense) poetry, have a sexual instinct, a sense of identity, integral beliefs – and then some other things too, like needs for nourishment and sleep, a capacity for laughter and for play, powers of reasoning and invention that are, by comparison with other terrestrial species, truly formidable, and more shared features yet – not substantial enough? Singly or together, these features all seem to be of some practical consequence. Consider only the sort of difference it might have made to their world if the beings called human were *not* susceptible to pain and humiliation. That would appear, so far as it is possible to think it through, to be a difference as substantial as any that are typically argued over when human nature is at issue: whether or not people are universally greedy and competitive, or are intrinsically moral, or are 'essentially' wedded to some larger hidden purpose or design.

We now know, in any case, how Rorty himself regards some of the human characteristics just collected – a collection shaped, indeed, according to his own especial emphases. And it is instructive to set those characteristics down side by side for a moment with the more radically historicist formulations he goes in for. One can do this by asking why people need ever actually be in pain, ever suffer or be oppressed. If they truly do just make up a nature for themselves, they could make up one that was proof against all that. It is hard to think why they have not done so, given how much suffering there has been all told. If we are machines, why do we not just 'invent the use for ourselves': reacting with joy or equanimity to (what formerly was) being tortured or being humiliated? Why not tinker with ourselves so that we will never, under any circumstances, be hungry? Or never feel weary under a burden of toil? Or cherish any belief or person so much as to be made vulnerable by doing that? Think how hard life would become for any would-be oppressor.[42] However, I do not genuinely mean any of this to be taken seriously. For it cannot.

There is, of course, *something* in it. People do find ways of making unavoidable suffering more bearable, forms of adaptation by which they seek to mitigate what they can of even the most brutal oppression, where it cannot be thrown off. Still, there are limits to human adaptability; and limits are part of what the discourse of human nature has been about. People can be pushed to, or close to, those limits and then they die or their lives become a torment. Or if they are a bit further back from the limits, their lives may be just harsh.

Where human beings find themselves in these sorts of situation, there at least a rhetoric of emancipation seems not entirely inappropriate. The idea is of a setting free from restraint or bondage: a setting free from restraint or bondage, here, of beings of a particular, not infinitely flexible, nature. How is this idea already useless, in a world where torture and hunger, political, religious, ethnic and other persecutions, are still rather prominent; where, as Richard Rorty for his part seems pretty well aware, large numbers of our species continue to live with, or under, social and political arrangements very far from comfortable?

The rhetoric of emancipation, it may be added, is not so distant from the rhetoric of 'utopia', which Rorty seems quite happy to employ. And even if the scope of the utopia projected by him may be less ambitious than the scope of many another – comfort simply and not the moon – there is an enormous, a world-transforming, amount to be said for that nonetheless, is there not?[43]

A final point. Rorty claims in one place to follow Sartre in this matter.[44] For Sartre, there is no human nature because 'Man is nothing else but that which he makes of himself' – he is 'a project . . . instead of being a kind of moss, or a fungus or a cauliflower'. So 'every one of us must choose himself', and that involves surpassing or widening, or else accommodating to, limitations of one kind and another.[45] Rorty's gloss on this is 'that man is always free to choose new descriptions (for, among other things, himself)'. The search for any putatively ultimate description or vocabulary, as he also contends, amounts to an attempt 'to escape from humanity'. That he should characterize it so is surely not surprising from a thinker who wants '[t]o say with Trilling that the mind is a poetry-making faculty'.[46]

I am reminded here, however, of other voices: most recently of Saul Bellow, writing about the genius of Mozart; and referring in this connection to our 'curious nature' and our 'inner freedom' with respect to the influence of external forces. And of Primo Levi, according to whom 'all of us are born poets' and 'the need to make poetry . . . is of all countries and all times'. And then, more distantly, of the young Marx's 'free, conscious activity'; and of the mature Marx's 'free development of every individual'. And of John Stuart Mill, reflecting on just how much Bentham overlooked in his too simple conception of 'man': on 'the love of *beauty*, the passion of the artist', and 'the love of *action*, the thirst for movement and activity'.

Yet Bellow is content to put what he says under the rubric of our 'trans-historical powers' and 'our common human nature'. Levi locates poetry amongst the 'activities to which we are predisposed genetically'. Marx invokes 'the forces . . . of humanity's own nature'. And Mill speaks likewise of 'these powerful constituents of human nature'. It is not clear to me that there is a difference of any substance between the idea they severally articulate – with whatever variations – and the Rorty-Sartre one.[47]

Notes

Bibliographical details for the works of Rorty referred to here, and the abbreviations used for them, may be found at p. 147.

1. ORT, p. 99.
2. See EHO, p. 1; Ths, pp. 564, 572, 578 n. 23; Fem, pp. 5, 12 n. 18.
3. CoP, p. 97. Cf. J.L. Austin, *Sense and Sensibilia*, Oxford 1962, p. 2.
4. CIS, pp. 4, 21; cf. p. 6.
5. EHO, p. 132.
6. CoP, p. 203; CIS, pp. 59, 60.
7. CIS, pp. 64, 185.
8. EHO, p. 77; Fem, p. 5.
9. CIS, p. xiii; ORT, p. 176.
10. Fem, p. 4.
11. CIS, p. 94.
12. See the text to note 4 above.
13. CIS, pp. 91–2.
14. CIS, p. 178.
15. CIS, p. 89.
16. CIS, p. 36 and n. 12.
17. See the text to note 8 above.
18. EHO, p. 18.

19. The *Guardian*, 13 March 1992, p. 25.
20. Ths, pp. 573 and 579 n. 28.
21. ORT, p. 197; EHO, p. 132.
22. EHO, pp. 144, 152.
23. ORT, p. 176.
24. Fem, p. 12 n. 22; CoP, p. 207.
25. CIS, p. 196; ORT, p. 211.
26. ORT, p. 213.
27. EHO, p. 132–3.
28. CIS, pp. xv, 74, 146, 173, 190, 197.
29. CIS, p. 89.
30. CIS, p. 65.
31. EHO, pp. 71–2.
32. EHO, pp. 74–5.
33. EHO, p. 78.
34. CIS, p. 192.
35. ORT, p. 213.
36. ORT, pp. 31, 22.
37. CIS, p. 35.
38. See the text to note 19 above.
39. Fem, p. 4; and see the text to note 10 above.
40. CIS, pp. 88–93.
41. CIS, pp. 187–8.
42. See the text to notes 22 and 35 above.
43. Cf. my 'Marxism and Moral Advocacy', in Norman Geras, *Discourses of Extremity*, London 1990, pp. 7–8.
44. ORT, p. 182 n. 17.
45. Jean-Paul Sartre, *Existentialism and Humanism*, London 1948 (reprinted 1966), pp. 27–9, 46.
46. PMN, pp. 361–2 n. 7, 377; CIS, p. 36.
47. 'Saul Bellow on Mozart', the *Guardian*, 2 April 1992, p. 25; Primo Levi, *The Mirror Maker*, London 1990, pp. 110–14; Karl Marx and Frederick Engels, *Collected Works*, London 1975, vol. 3, p. 276; Karl Marx, *Capital*, vol. 1, Harmondsworth 1976, p. 739; Marx, *Grundrisse*, Harmondsworth 1973, p. 488; J.S. Mill, 'Bentham', in Mary Warnock, ed., *Utilitarianism*, London 1962, pp. 100–101.

3

Community and Dissociation

'Whatever hope is yours,/Was my life also.'
Wilfred Owen

Human solidarity – but no common humanity. Humanism – but without any human nature. Widowed figures, so to say, out of the work of Richard Rorty. In what follows I enquire how well they fare like this.

Earlier I documented the disparity between the ways of thought of the Righteous Among the Nations, the people who rescued Jews during the Holocaust, and Rorty's hypothesis about them. Where he speculates on parochial forms of identification having been usual amongst rescuers, they themselves give voice to universalist attachments, of exactly the kind that Rorty for his part holds to be weak or even impossible.[1]

There is, now, a further issue I want to pursue in this same connection. For Rorty appears to find no difficulty, in the very essay in which he forswears a 'universalistic attitude', in affirming his commitment to human solidarity.[2] More lately, as one of the lecturers in the 1993 Oxford Amnesty series on 'Human Rights', he has affirmed also the culture of human rights. This culture is, Rorty says, a 'welcome fact of the post-Holocaust world'; it is 'morally superior to other cultures'.[3] Such affirmations are part of the more general viewpoint he recommends to us: the viewpoint of a liberalism without philosophical foundations; of support for the project of a

71

democratic utopia on the basis of historical contingencies only. Human solidarity, human rights and plain humanism, but without recourse to any underlying universalist notion or principle which might 'ground' them – these are from that same stable.

In the present chapter, I shall seek to vindicate the ways of thought of the rescuers as being more suitable to a democratic ethic and practice. I shall argue that what Rorty offers us is not compelling – indeed it is not coherent – as an alternative.

I

I start by coming back to a statement I have had occasion to refer to already in Chapter 1. The statement, from Rorty's essay 'Solidarity', concerns how American liberals are to react to the hopeless and miserable lives of some of their young black compatriots. Should the latter be helped because they are 'fellow human beings'? One may, Rorty allows, say that; 'but it is much more persuasive,' he thinks, 'morally as well as politically, to describe them as our fellow *Americans* – to insist that it is outrageous that an *American* should live without hope.'[4] I would understand this better, I have to say, if the point of concern were that these black Americans were having to live without something else, like American passports for example. But hope? Is hope specific to Americans, or more important to them than it is to other sorts of people? The line of thought is so unpromising that I at once abandon it.

Rorty's statement, it may be, is not about hope so much as it is about outrage, about the sources of moral offence. But is it more offensive morally that Americans should live without hope than that non-Americans should? Why, if they do not have a special national claim on hope? Perhaps an American liberal will just care more about Americans without hope; as I might for my part feel more acutely the injustice committed against me or one of mine, a loved one, friend or other intimate, than I feel a similar injustice inflicted elsewhere. The thing is then more upsetting, more distressing, or more devastating, as the case may be. However, to commend this as the source of a greater moral persuasiveness . . . ? If we insist that what makes having to live without hope outrageous is that it is an American – or, generalizing, a member of our own national community – who suffers the misfortune, do we not thereby also say that it is not outrageous when the same misfortune befalls the members of some other national community?

How far does that go? To live without hope is bad enough. But let the bonds of community be urged as determining what is outrageous, what is morally persuasive, and it will then be hard to know why it matters when members of another community are being tortured or enslaved. The reach of community and community loyalty, moreover, is variable. An American may indeed care more about fellow Americans – just so long as they are not blacks, or Jews, or others she does not feel to be of her 'own kind'. Rorty thinks to have identified here the sensibilities of people who rescued Jews during the Holocaust. But what he identifies leads by the shortest of routes to the outlook of their persecutors and murderers.

And yet. Rorty is not of that outlook. Have I misunderstood him? I do not think so, but let us take things a bit more slowly. I return to another proposition of his already referred to in Chapter 1. Listing some of the narrower types of grouping which for him properly exemplify the notion 'one of us' – such as a 'Greek like ourselves', or a 'fellow Catholic' – Rorty writes:

> I want to deny that 'one of us human beings' (as opposed to animals, vegetables, and machines) can have the same sort of force as any of the previous examples. I claim that the force of 'us' is, typically, contrastive in the sense that it contrasts with a 'they' which is also made up of human beings – the wrong sort of human beings.

73

A little further on in the essay, directly following the 'fellow Americans' statement, he says similarly:

> The point of these examples is that our sense of solidarity is strongest when those with whom solidarity is expressed are thought of as 'one of us', where 'us' means something smaller and more local than the human race. That is why 'because she is a human being' is a weak, unconvincing explanation of a generous action.[5]

Now, these observations do not concern only the relative ease or difficulty of what Rorty goes on in the same place to call 'imaginative identification'. They appear to be intended also as specifying the bounds of 'moral obligation'.[6] This appearance is confirmed elsewhere in Rorty's work, at other points at which the idea of 'being one of us', of community membership, is put forward by him as of crucial practical import. Thus, not just the privilege of solidarity but, in the view he endorses in *Philosophy and the Mirror of Nature*, even 'personhood is a matter of "being one of us" . . . rather than a feature of certain organisms to be isolated by empirical means.'[7] Likewise, moral prohibitions against hurting babies (and 'the better looking sorts of animals') are not grounded, he says, in their possession of feeling. 'It is, if anything, the other way round. The moral prohibitions are expressions of a sense of community based on the imagined possibility of conversation, and the attribution of feelings is little more than a reminder of these prohibitions.' Since Hegel, Rorty suggests, 'philosophers [have] begun toying with the notion that the individual apart from his society is just one more animal.'[8]

Given what has gone before, I take Rorty's own version of this toyed-with notion not merely in the sense of the uncontroversial truth that a member of the human species must be socialized within a community of other humans in order to acquire the cultural attributes of humanity. I take it as stating that any (putative) person's claim to moral consideration depends, like personhood itself, on 'being one of us', being *of* the community. Consider what becomes, for Rorty, of human dignity: '[T]he naturalized Hegelian analogue of "intrinsic human dignity" is the comparative dignity of a group with which a person identifies herself. Nations or churches or movements are, on this view, shining historical examples not because they reflect rays emanating from a higher source, but because of contrast-effects – comparisons with other, worse communities. Persons have dignity not as an interior luminescence, but because they share in such contrast-effects.'[9] Let us put aside for the moment the limited nature of the choice this passage offers us: a share in human dignity either because one is part of a given – better – group, or else on account of some higher, or luminescent, in any event plainly dubious, metaphysical source. Let us put aside the question why such a share of dignity might not just be allowed on the basis that, as the member of *any* old human group, one will have some important things in common with the members of the better group. I want first to pose another question. Doesn't Rorty's view have seriously anti-democratic implications?

Well, I think it does. But more interestingly here perhaps, Rorty also thinks so; or at any rate he thought so when he wrote *Philosophy and the Mirror of Nature*. For that is what he says about this view which philosophers have been toying with since Hegel; he speaks, precisely, of its 'antidemocratic implications' (in connection with their effect on the reception of Hegelian modes of thought within analytic philosophy).[10] It seems hard, indeed, to embrace the view and to evade the implications. If an individual's moral status, whether as the bearer of human dignity or of personhood, or as the beneficiary of moral prohibitions against being hurt, is to rest only on the going sense of community, this will surely serve to underwrite every discourse of exclusion under the sun.

And yet. Rorty would seem to think it possible to evade the anti-democratic implications of the view of which he says they are the implications. How? The answer may seem obvious: we need only to extend our sense of community. So he proposes in the essay 'Solidarity'. '[M]y position', he writes, 'is *not* incompatible with urging that we try to extend our sense of "we" to people whom we have previously thought of as "they".' Doing that, one may continue to employ the vocabulary of 'human solidarity', but at the same time 'disengage it from what [have] often been thought of as its "philosophical presuppositions".'[11] Again: 'The right way to take the slogan "We have obligations to human beings simply as such" is as a means of reminding ourselves to keep trying to expand our sense of "us" as far as we can'; on the other hand, 'If one reads it [the slogan] the wrong way, one will think of our "common humanity" . . . as a "philosophical foundation" for democratic politics.'[12] Finally:

> *We* have to start from where *we* are – that is part of the force of [Wilfrid] Sellars's claim that we are under no obligations other than the 'we-intentions' of the communities with which we identify. What takes the curse off this ethnocentrism is not that the largest such group is 'humanity' or 'all rational beings' – no one, I have been claiming, *can* make *that* identification – but, rather, that it is the ethnocentrism of a 'we' ('we liberals') which is dedicated to enlarging itself, to creating an ever larger and more variegated *ethnos*. It is the 'we' of the people who have been brought up to distrust ethnocentrism.[13]

II

From radically communitarian and apparently anti-universalist premisses, then, we get human solidarity – and in an outlook which Rorty is also happy on occasion to call 'humanist',[14] and to connect, most recently, with the culture of human rights (a point to which I shall later return). I suggest now some reasons for finding this resolution unpersuasive.

i) If you cannot get there, then you cannot get there. Getting nearer there is not the same thing. Or else you can get there.

If, as Rorty insists, the force of any 'we', any sense of moral community, must depend on the contrast with a human 'they', on enclosing something smaller and more local than the human race; if someone's just being part of humankind gives at best a weak reason for treating them generously, at worst no possible basis at all for imaginative identification and moral concern; then you can make 'we' larger, but you cannot make it large enough to get rid of the aforesaid ethnocentric curse.

Starting, for instance, from fellow Americans, you might begin to extend your sense of 'we' to Mexicans, Brazilians, Chileans and so forth, and thence to the peoples of Europe. Or starting from fellow Catholics, you might move on to every kind of Christian, then to Jews and Muslims. But this process either stops short somewhere within humankind, on account of the needed contrast-effects, or it does not. If it does, then some people, the people of Africa perhaps, or Hindus and atheists, get to be excluded from moral concern and they can go hungry or be massacred for all you care. Strange humanism. Strange human rights. It is not easy to see, indeed, how the curse *can* be taken off an idea of moral community resting on a contrast-effect like the 'wrong sort of human beings' – at least where this is supposed to govern not whose company you keep but who has human dignity or might 'deserve to be saved'.[15] On the other hand, if the process of extending your sense of 'we' does not stop short, then you will get there after all: to a sense of 'we' capable of encompassing all humanity. But the conclusion will have cancelled the premiss. This was therefore no good. You will have found that in the end you do not need, for some of the most important kinds of moral consideration anyway, that intra-human contrast-effect.

In a nutshell, if the conception really is humanist or liberal in any attractive meaning of these terms, it is so only by virtue of reaching a destination it declares to be unattainable.

ii) There are in any case some questionable assumptions at work here concerning 'imaginative identification', the inclusion of others within one's range of sympathy and moral reckoning; assumptions having to do with both the scope and the nature of such identification.

Consider, first, why it might be thought impossible to identify with all of humanity. Perhaps it is because the sheer size of this particular set, or the wide geographical distribution of its members, puts it beyond the reach of even the largest mental and emotional capacity. Humanity is just not small or local enough. But think again of Rorty's 'fellow Americans'. They are some 250 million people, scattered across half a continent. And since Rorty himself allows that a sense of 'we' can be extended at least somewhat, think of its being extended from these fellow Americans only as far as Mexicans and Brazilians; or only as far as Chinese. In all now, this is in the region of either 500 or 1400 million people. Such numbers are, to be sure, still smaller than the more than 5 thousand million of the current world population. But that cannot affect the present point. You either can identify, in a certain meaning and despite the size of this 'community', with fellow Americans plus whoever; in which case you can identify with humanity also. Or else, for reasons of size, you cannot identify with humanity, and then nor can you with Americans plus whoever. It is just not credible that the significant threshold in this matter, where compassion and solicitude will go no further, lies somewhere beyond several hundred million people.

The real issue concerns the meaning of identification. For this may, but it also need not, be about smallness or locale. There is a sense in which I have an identification with my immediate family that I could not possibly have with all humanity. It has something to do with the detail and the density, the presence, of lived relationships, a strongly felt sense of my place within this close network of them, a depth of caring about and loving these particular persons, and so on. Let us say that my family is for me the most 'concrete' of communities; it can be, all of its members, vivid to my mind and my emotions more or less simultaneously. Humanity is not like that, not for me, not for anyone. But nor is any enormously large human aggregate.[16] Americans imaginatively identifying with fellow Americans (as anyone else with their compatriots) identify in a different sense and way, not with a comparable immediacy. The threads of identification are thinner. These might include, for example, the fact of speaking a common language or of being governed under the same constitution; of being proud and/or critical of similar historical traditions; of liking baseball, jazz, Walt Whitman; of just being known, even, as 'an American'. Here as elsewhere, concreteness or thickness comes, if it comes at all, out of more slender connections, each one an 'abstraction'. Just so, I might identify also with people across the planet from me, other writers or teachers, other socialists, other Jews.

But equally, just so, one can identify with people, anywhere, irrespective of their professional, political, ethnic or other identity. The threads, the abstractions, will merely be different ones. They may look like this: 'He is worried for the future of his children; she is unable to pursue her vocation; they are struggling to pay for the medicines they need'. Or like this: 'They cannot say freely what they think; they are afraid of being seized; they are hungry, exhausted, in pain.' On the other hand: 'They are fighting against injustice, trying to change things for the better; they want better schools; they want playing fields.' Or again: 'The community itself, all that these people hold dear, is threatened. They are living without hope.'

Consider, now, the following locution, as coming from one woman to another: 'We should help them; they are women.' I do not think this unrealistic either morally or psychologically in the way of encouraging solidarity and support. Its persuasive force, though, would plainly not be due to any smallness or geographical concentration of the set 'women'. So what would it be due to? Would it be the bare fact of a shared identity and implicit contrast-effect – as if the expression said only, 'They are like *us* (not like those others)'? I may not be in an ideal position to judge here but I do dare to suggest that there is something else to it, something substantive about the

79

identity invoked. It is that, as women, those on behalf of whom the support is elicited are likely to be able to use support: whether because, as women, they are not likely to have been favoured with social advantages, or because, as these particular women, they are known to be especially burdened and oppressed in ways that women typically are, or are known to be especially vulnerable to, or the victims already of, male violence. The appeal in other words, I am suggesting, albeit spoken by a woman and on behalf of other women, carries a moral freight of a rather more general kind; such that, why, even a man might be able to find himself moved by it.

In case that should seem doubtful, consider instead an appeal encouraging identification and help without any shared identity being invoked – not in direct 'one-of-us' mode anyway. Consider, as coming from an adult, the appeal, 'We should do something; they are (only) children.' Again, I just take it this carries some persuasive force. Perhaps part of the reason it does is that, having all been and still knowing children, we can identify with them, although children ourselves no longer. But another part, I contend, has to do with a particular fact we know and feel about children; it has to do with their vulnerability. On account of this, however, children may be taken as simply highlighting what is a possibility for anyone, any human being: the possibility in virtue of his natural needs and limitations, in virtue of her acquired values, loves or hopes, of being hurt. In that respect all human beings are potentially children. They can be made very easily to suffer – innocently, for nothing. If you can respond with sympathy and generosity to someone merely because he is a child, then so can you respond merely because she is a human being, because of her general human traits. The present discussion begins from the Righteous Among the Nations, rescuers who risked a great deal on behalf of others. But change the focus and the scale. What on earth motivates supporters of Amnesty International today? Do we say that people should not be locked away for their beliefs, should not be tortured, because (that is *if*) they are fellow city-dwellers? Or fellow academics, baseball-lovers, nationals even?

iii) For Rorty, remember, it is the wrong way to think about human solidarity and reciprocal moral obligation if we take our 'common humanity' as a philosophical presupposition or foundation.[17] This is just one of many such judgements, the recurring signature of his anti-foundationalism. Thus, 'the disappearance of the transcendental subject – of "man" as something having a nature which society can repress or understand' Rorty describes as being of no inferential consequence for human solidarity; a sense of human solidarity is 'ungroundable'. Or, again, it has no 'source': 'the idea of human solidarity is simply the fortunate happenstance creation of modern times'. Liberal political freedoms equally, *pace* Habermas, do not require any 'consensus about what is universally human'.[18]

This renunciation of so-called foundations yields some bizarre results, becoming at the limit a renunciation more simply of reasons. Here, for example, Rorty tries to meet an anticipated objection to his view that persons have 'human' dignity just as a function of the contrast-effects they benefit from through membership of some given, putatively superior, community. He writes:

> The . . . objection is that on my view a child found wandering in the woods, the remnant of a slaughtered nation whose temples have been razed and whose books have been burned, has no share in human dignity. This is indeed a consequence, but it does not follow that she may be treated like an animal. For it is part of the tradition of *our* community that the human stranger from whom all dignity has been stripped is to be taken in, to be reclothed with dignity.[19]

Notice in passing a certain 'softening' of what Rorty accepts as being indeed a consequence of his view. For, of course, according to that view it would not necessarily be only the destruction of her nation that stripped this wandering child of all dignity. Should the nation in question happen to be of a worse or the wrong sort, her membership of it while it was thriving would already leave her, if found wandering, bereft. But I am more interested here in how Rorty would have us turn back from what his softened consequence otherwise seems to permit and threaten. We may not treat the child like an animal because . . . well, because it is not 'our' tradition to do so.

This is to commend the form, having evacuated it of its content. It is to give the tradition itself as a reason after reject-ing the reasons of the tradition. It is first to put forth, as your own view, matter challenging, casting aside, the com-ponent principles and arguments of another given view; which latter you then uphold nevertheless as being, quite generally, 'our' view. Let us tell a different story about the nation from which this wandering child has come: a story belonging to the time before the nation's temples were razed and its books burned.

There was a certain Elder of that nation who was much honoured within it, for it was known that a long time ago he had done something particularly brave and heroic by which many had been saved from a ghastly fate. It was the belief in this place that such acts ought to be honoured, it being widely understood how hard it was to bring oneself to take the kind of risks the Elder took and how awful it would be to suffer the kind of fate from which he had saved people. But it happened one day that a man from within this same community began to claim there was no reliable evidence for what the Elder was reputed to have done – there was indeed good evidence that he had stolen the credit for an act of his sister's – and even had it been the Elder's doing anyway, so this man said, it was not the sort of thing that should be honoured. It was better, more persuasive, to honour prudence and caution than courage or heroism. Courage, he said, was a feeble, maybe even an unhealthy, impulse.

Digesting his critical views, some within the community now expressed their intention not to turn out again on the annual Day of the Elder. The critic himself, however, admonished them. They should continue to honour the old man. Those admonished turned to the critic, surprised. Why should they? They expected he would perhaps give them some other or new reason; though they understood from things he had said in the past that certain kinds of reason were excluded. Honouring someone on account merely of their age, for instance, he would surely not recommend, nor honouring them just for the sake of the ceremony. He had often given it out that age was not a useful notion at all and the belief in ceremony as such he regularly disparaged as a rather pathetic sort of security-blanket of people he liked to call 'essentialists'. So, why?, they all wondered. And this is what he said to them. 'It is part of *our* tradition', he said, 'to honour courageous acts on behalf of those in danger.' A few from amongst his audience at this point drifted off alleging that the terms in which he spoke just covertly resurrected the very reasons he had lately been debunking. But we shall sturdily ignore these cynics for the time being in order to return to the child.

We have found her wandering in the woods. A young man amongst us (who has not read Peter Singer) says, 'Look at this animal. Let's kill her; or keep her in a cage.' For the benefit of the rest of the group, mostly shocked at his suggestion, the young man then sets out a number of the ideas he has, ideas which have been learned from his Mentor who is also present at the scene. The young man says it is the wrong approach to the notions of solidarity and moral obligation if we think of our 'common humanity' – he indicates the scare-quotes by gesturing with his fingers – as a presupposition or foundation for them. He has 'given up the Enlightenment assumption', he says, of 'something ahistorical, something common to all human beings qua human'. Or else, as he also says – again with the fingers, to accompany the first word – '"humanity" is a biological rather than a moral notion.'[20] The child, he points out, is not an American (the nationality, as it happens, of our group); she is from a much worse kind of nation and so has no dignity. Not being one of us, she is not even a person

83

really. Since he cannot conjure up any sense of community with her ('I mean, listen to the noises she makes; you couldn't converse with her; she doesn't even speak a proper language'), the young man does not see how there could be any moral prohibition against hurting her.

However, the Mentor intervenes now. He says the child may on no account be harmed. It is out of the question. The young man cannot understand this. He got all those ideas of his precisely from the Mentor. They seem to undermine the reasons for not mistreating the child. The Mentor, he knows, will not appeal, either, to various other notions still sometimes deployed in support of a universalist ethic – such as that we and the child are creatures of the same God and He forbids us to harm her, or that there is an eternal Law of Nature embodying an ethic for all human beings. What could be the Mentor's reason, then, for ruling out the proposed course of action? The young man waits. And the Mentor simply says this: that it is part of the tradition of *our* community – he gestures with his arms as if to encompass the group – that the human stranger is to be taken in. Apart from the young man himself who stands there confused, the rest of the group applaud the Mentor for his intervention. We think it is to his credit. Still, some are inclined to wonder whether it is any credit to the things he has taught the young man. For the terms of his intervention, these people suggest, covertly resurrect the very reasons the Mentor has, through those teachings, debunked. In favour of their suggestion, the same people argue, is his use of the phrase 'the human stranger'. What, they ask, could be the burden of it other than to encourage us to regard the child as one of us just because of what she shares with us 'qua human' – given that, qua stranger, she is plainly *not* one of us? But I ignore these doubters too for the time being.

I ignore them not because they do not have a point but because I want to follow through another possibility before us here: the possibility, namely, that so far from wishing to resurrect what he has seemingly renounced, Rorty might be quite happy to affirm merely 'our tradition' itself, or the contingencies that have made it ours, in support of acting or forbearing to act in certain ways. We may consider what this does for the tradition so affirmed.

We have seen that he thinks it compatible with the overtly parochialist viewpoints he puts forward, to urge us to extend our sense of 'we' to more and more people. Of this expansive, solidary impulse – 'characteristic of liberals' – Rorty insists:

> [It] rests on nothing deeper than the historical contingencies . . . which brought about the development of the moral and political vocabularies typical of the secularized democratic societies of the West. As this vocabulary has been de-theologized and de-philosophized, 'human solidarity' has emerged as a powerful piece of rhetoric. I have no wish to diminish its power, but only to disengage it from what [have] often been thought of as its 'philosophical presuppositions'.[21]

About 'an ideal liberal society' he writes, similarly:

> It is a society whose hero is the strong poet and the revolutionary because it recognizes that it is what it is, has the morality it has, speaks the language it does, not because it approximates the will of God or the nature of man but because certain poets and revolutionaries of the past spoke as they did.[22]

From the first of these two passages we have, instead of the 'tradition' of before, more pluralistically, a set of 'moral and political vocabularies'. But this difference is not material to the author's principal intention in such passages. Let us now think about his 'nothing-deeper' basis for solidarity. I shall assume, in turn, that it is only that the various contingencies have made our tradition or vocabularies *ours* that provides this basis, and that it is the contingencies themselves that provide it.

So, first: the fact is invoked of a tradition's being our tradition or a vocabulary's being one of our vocabularies. It is invoked as of itself sufficient by way of justification for some act or prohibition. But if we are not then also given something in favour of the content of this tradition or vocabulary, we are given in effect no more than a name. It is as if we were to be told that we may not, or we must, act in a certain way because of *The Word*. Or it is to be offered *Our View* as a reason without any reason for *Our View*; or without any reason from within *Our View* such as to make it actually a view and not an incantation. Perhaps there are traditions which this style of exhortation models, but it scarcely seems apt to the traditions Richard Rorty wants to call his own. Appealing to the authority of mere forms or titles, it is a style that sits ill beside either the secular or the democratic habits of mind he would more generally encourage. And it sits oddly within a tradition disinclined to appeal to the authority of tradition as such, preferring the ways of deliberative reflection and reasoned advocacy. Is it not a Pyrrhic defence of the moral and intellectual legacy of humanist liberalism to fall back on such a style of exhortation?

Rorty speaks of the powerful rhetoric of human solidarity. He has no wish to diminish it; he would only disengage it from its presumed philosophical presuppositions. The argument of this chapter is that he does thereby precisely diminish it – if rhetorical power, at least, has anything at all to do with procedures of persuasive reasoning. Perhaps, though, it is another kind of potency he has in mind. Under the star of nothing-deeper contingency we do seem to ride the borderlands of the mysterious. That something is 'our tradition', for example, must either work as a general type of justification or else not. If the former, then it can justify not taking in as well as taking in the wandering child, reacting to lives of hopelessness with indifference rather than outrage, and so on. If instead of a 'huddled masses' liberal you get to be speaking to a Ku Klux Klan xenophobe and racist, or even to a 'Couldn't-care-less' conservative or aesthete and ironist, or to an apolitical jock, 'our tradition' can yield not only black but also white. It can yield, indeed, anything whatsoever, since traditions are created as well as continued. We may spare Rorty this particular outcome by opting for the other alternative: that 'our tradition' is not a general justification but applies only to traditions that are *his*.[23] But we have already been here. For either, now, we may expect to be given something relevant about the content of the traditions in question, something – in place of the renounced presuppositions – telling specifically in favour of these traditions, or we are left only with the naked word 'Ours'. Naked and magical: working, darkly, for us but not for them.[24]

Second: not the fact itself of a tradition's being ours but some contingency associated with this fact is invoked. It might be, as in the second of the two passages above, that 'certain poets and revolutionaries of the past spoke as they did'. We encounter, in this second passage, a typical Rortian posture. It gives us but two options: on the one hand, God or a surrogate for God, some hidden design or purpose (what 'the nature of man' here is probably meant to suggest) unfolding across history; on the other hand, mere accident. As the hard-nosed secular folk we must surely be, what choice then do we have? Notice, however, that, as I have already indicated, the context of the passage is one in which Rorty purports to be talking about an *ideal* liberal society. He *commends* it to us, therefore, in such terms; commends its heroes as his heroes, commends 'the morality it has' as his own. But one may legitimately wonder in that case why, leaving God and all teleology out of it, we will not be able to find any other, indeed 'deeper', basis than mere accident, any better *reason* than that, for upholding our traditions and our values: maybe for instance, beyond the fact that some poets and revolutionaries spoke as they did, something in what they actually said and in the reasons why they said it – assuming these did not just also come down to certain, even earlier, poets having spoken as *they* did.

To proffer on behalf of a tradition or moral viewpoint nothing deeper, which is to say no more, than an extrinsic feature of it, does not seem a significant or even genuinely secularizing improvement on the kind of metaphysical supports with which Rorty hopes to embarrass imagined interlocutors. It calls upon some strange secret inhering in adventitious circumstances; quite as though I were to explain that I have long been in favour of public health provision because I once saw the words 'public health provision' written in bold letters on a wall. A secret lurks here somewhere, for once again this kind of nothing-deeper basis will either justify anything – via a different wall, other poets and revolutionaries, and certain counter-revolutionaries, why not? – or it will justify only *our* tradition or viewpoint. Whichever the case, it belongs then truly to the mysteries, such a power to generate stark logical contradictions, or such another, special power, the exclusive, unexplained possession of you and me.

Finally, in fact, possession of you *or* me. The end result will be not only (as Rorty may be happy to concede)[25] a 'We-just-do' kind of liberalism, ranged assertively against the world. It will be so many 'I-just-do' voices within liberalism, disintegrating fragments as it were, not so much continuing a conversation as keeping up the noise. Few traditions are completely uniform or monolithic, and liberalism in particular prides itself on its diversity. One feature of this diversity is that Rorty's own brand of liberalism is more radical, more congenial and more . . . (actually) humane than certain other liberalisms which come to mind. The constituent voices of liberalism, however, can be no better off in the resources of persuasion than the tradition as a whole. With nothing but contingencies, a multiplicity of random and dubiously relevant circumstances to turn to, those voices would do equally well simply blurting back and forth, 'I just do'. It is hard to see here, in this possibility we have now finished following through, an appealing vision of the liberal tradition.

Is it a fair one, though? Can it really be fair to present Rorty thus, with no more to urge on behalf of human solidarity or of liberalism than that such are our traditions, or such the contingencies which have made them ours? The answer is both yes and no. Yes, because this is what he says when it suits him to, which is frequently. I believe we are entitled to take him then at his word, in order to explore the implications of what he says as a serious line of thought. But also no, it is not altogether fair. For Rorty does have something more to urge in favour of solidarity and of liberalism.

iv) What he has to urge is the idea of a common humanity. It is the same idea, that is, which he also likes to dismiss, as being just one amongst various unnecessary philosophical presuppositions or foundations. The doubters from my two stories did after all have a point: what is dismissed gets resurrected; a 'ground' that was lost is again found. And though it is not *altogether* fair, consequently, to take Rorty as invoking only our tradition and associated contingencies when he leans as well on the notion of a human nature, it is not altogether *unfair* either, because by his own lights he ought not to lean on that, and so we may legitimately enquire what his position would look like if he didn't in fact lean on it. But anyway he does.

Notwithstanding his many denials of a common human nature, notwithstanding repeated assertions by him of a human variability virtually without limit – the most extreme example of which comes in one of his more recent statements, recommending to us 'a picture of human beings as children of their time and place, without any significant metaphysical or biological [!] limits on their plasticity'[26] – Rorty does put forward a universalist basis for extensive liberal solidarity. For he relies on the existence of some common characteristics in human beings. His emphasis in this may change: resting now upon characteristics common both to human beings and to other animals, as with the susceptibility to pain; and now upon characteristics common only to human beings, as with the susceptibility to humiliation or the capacity for language and poetry. But setting his face, either way, against cruelty and the countenancing of avoidable human suffering, he falls back on the fact of human beings having a nature, both animal and human; one which, it seems then perfectly possible to say, can be 'repressed'.[27] Or it can be crushed, or violated, wantonly disregarded in pursuit of one sectional advantage or another.

When all is said and done, *that* is what Rorty resurrects in encouraging us to think about solidarity 'as the ability to see more and more traditional differences (of tribe, religion, race, customs, and the like) as unimportant when compared with similarities with respect to pain and humiliation'.[28] As this central, vitiating self-contradiction in his work was discussed at some length in Chapter 2, I shall not further rehearse its details here, except to comment on a specific peculiarity arising from one side of it and which is germane in the present context.

I put it in the form of a simple question. Is there not something rather implausible about insisting on the communal sources of strong solidarity, and insisting at the same time on the irrelevance of the idea of a common humanity to the goal of more expansive solidaristic relations? Insisting on the first, on the fact that bonds of mutual sympathy will tend to be more powerful the smaller and more local is the human group in question, one says that it is easier to feel for and act in support of those with whom we have *most* in common. But insisting on the second, claiming that it is of no consequence for human solidarity if we can no longer avail ourselves of the notion of '"man" as something having a nature . . .', claiming that the vocabulary of human solidarity is not at all diminished by being disengaged from such a presupposition,[29] one says in effect that the most wide-ranging, tendentially global, kind of solidarity is conceivable even though the beings to be brought into closer affective union by it do not all have *anything whatsoever* in common.

That they do not is, of course, absurd, and this is why Rorty, like everybody else who ever says they do not, cannot maintain it consistently, recurring when need be to the likes of pain or humiliation or sundry other human uniformities. But should we, in stubbornly literal-minded spirit, just accept the saying of it at face value and ignore the taking of it back, then we are asked to believe – so to say in the first part – that solidarity nourishes itself, receives its strength and vigour, from commonalities which are concrete, palpable, lived; and asked

90

also to believe – in the second part – that feelings of extensive mutual sympathy can be created amongst beings who, of almost infinite plasticity, may share with very large numbers of other such beings no common features at all. Granted, there is nothing here to say that there may not still be amongst these beings all sorts of purely contingent, criss-crossing similarities: this, that or whatever, linking some of the beings to others in haphazard ways. Nevertheless, if what we are asked to believe in the first part is really so, then would it not be a better basis for extensive solidarity that, beyond any traits they shared contingently, these beings started just qua humans with something substantial in common? As, in point of actual fact, they do.[30]

v) Not only in this particular but in a more general way as well Rorty fails to see the relevance and potential force of the consideration that people share a common nature. The more general failure to see it comes with the theme, pervading all his writings, that human solidarity, repugnance for cruelty, the holding of moral positions of any kind, is not actually a matter of having cogent reasons. Against such a backdrop, it will appear less surprising perhaps if 'our tradition', 'certain poets' and so forth, can be proposed by him to be as good a basis as any for deciding how to conduct oneself. This sort of nothing-deeper contingency will be deep enough, for there *is* no genuine depth. In the absence of any real reasons of force to constitute it, one settles for sentiment, and sentiment can as well attach itself to tradition as such, the word of a poet, indeed anything, as it can to the dignity of strangers or to the existence of a common humanity.

Here is the theme. 'I do not think there are any plain moral facts out there in the world,' Rorty writes, '. . . nor any neutral ground on which to stand and argue that either torture or kindness are preferable to the other.'[31] There is 'no noncircular theoretical backup for the belief that cruelty is horrible', 'no *neutral*, noncircular way to defend the liberal's claim that cruelty is the worst thing we do'.[32] You 'can want to relieve suffering without having an interesting answer when Socrates asks you *why* you desire this';[33] likewise, it may be 'enough just to *prefer* democratic societies'.[34] We should, accordingly, 'simply drop the distinction between rational judgement and cultural bias'.[35] 'Rationality, when viewed as the formation of syllogisms based on the discovery of "the facts" and the application of such principles as "Pain should be minimized" . . . is a myth.'[36] Not rationality, enquiry or theory, but imagination and various genres of narrative – 'ethnography, the journalist's report, the comic book, the docudrama, and, especially, the novel' – are the medium of moral persuasion and conviction.[37] So, 'there is no way to "refute" a sophisticated, consistent, passionate psychopath – for example, a Nazi who would favour his own elimination if he himself turned out to be Jewish'; 'demonstration' is not available in such matters. But one might still attempt to 'convert' the Nazi. One could try to 'show him how nice things can be in free societies, how horrible things are in the Nazi camps'. One would be making use in doing so of 'the urge to redescribe' which is 'the wisdom of the novel' (although this wisdom, it has to be said, also 'encompasses a sense of how Hitler might be seen as in the right and the Jews in the wrong').[38]

In his Amnesty Human Rights lecture, Rorty expresses it like this. He says that 'most of the work of changing moral intuitions is . . . done by manipulating our feelings', and that 'the emergence of the human rights culture seems to owe nothing to increased moral knowledge, and everything to hearing sad and sentimental stories.' He says: 'The best . . . argument for putting foundationalism behind us is . . . [that it] would be more efficient to do so, because it would let us concentrate our energies on manipulating sentiments, on sentimental education . . . [which] acquaints people of different kinds with one another . . .' The suggestion to extend respect to people universally 'has never been backed up by an argument based on neutral premises, and it never will be'. What it depends on rather, Rorty holds, is 'sympathy' – 'the sort that white Americans had more of after reading *Uncle Tom's Cabin* than before, the sort that we have more of after watching TV programmes about the genocide in Bosnia'.[39]

Let me respond by first registering two points of agreement. I agree with Rorty that no neutral, demonstrable, knock-down argument is available on behalf of wide solidarity (or of humanism, liberalism, socialism etc.) against anyone starting from normative premises radically antithetical to the ones usual in this ethico-political domain. In face of an opponent for whom it is just axiomatic that the members of one or another group are not due any consideration for their pain, fall outside the circle of mutual obligation and respect, can be freely used and beaten, can or even should be killed, and so on, argument may well be futile. So may it be also against someone who self-consciously chooses to live out a life of profligate cruelty and destructiveness, randomly distributed. I do not deploy against Rorty, because I do not subscribe to, an ethical naturalism or the like, according to which our moral values are to be had more or less deductively from the realities of the world, so that the perpetrators of evil must be then either ignorant or illogical. They may be, but that is something else. For it could also be that the axiomatic bases from which they start are different, and bad.

Second, sympathy, sentiment, imagination, and equally the cultural genres, to say nothing of the modes of living, which educate them, plainly do matter greatly to the sort of generic moral outlook Rorty shares with most of his readers. No amount of argument from principle, no effort of purely rationalist inference from general norms to particular courses of action, will make up for the lack in anyone of elementary feeling – whether this be of compassion for the suffering of others or of antipathy towards the callous causing of it. The place of sentiment within moral consciousness is not to be doubted or underestimated.

We are not, however, bound by the narrow options Rorty sometimes seems to want to present us with here. Even if there is no knock-down, altogether unanswerable demonstration on the basis of premises acceptable to everyone that kindness is preferable to torture, or democracy to persecution and genocide, this does not mean we are left helplessly incapable of distinguishing between weighty reasons, on the one hand, and mere arbitrariness, eccentricity or accident on the other. Rorty risks falling into the trap against which he constantly warns his 'metaphysicians': of thinking reason can only be that if it is completely overwhelming, an omnipotent power.

Thus, though there may be no logical necessity about this, it is widely the case all the same (and *not* only within our culture) that basic codes of moral conduct and deliberations about what may or may not rightly be done relate in definite, if not always direct, ways to considerations of suffering – the avoidance and alleviation of it – and to the promotion and maintenance of well-being, in the largest sense. This is the type of consideration which nearly anyone can understand as the possible candidate for a compelling, action-guiding reason, because in the experience of everyone will be some kind of knowledge, albeit of variable breadth, depth and sensitivity, of what suffering and well-being actually feel like. We can go further than this. There is *already* here a tendency, however restricted it may sometimes be, towards generalization, a generalization beyond the self to others. For not only has the self been formed, and is it permanently constituted, in a context of others, so that its most fundamental notions about suffering and well-being cannot but embrace (some of) those others, their hurts and their flourishing being partly determinative of its own. The very processes, too, of practical deliberation, the thinking and enjoining and persuading in terms of rules or norms of conduct, only make sense in relation to some given generality of actors and instances.

This generality could, in logic, stop at the boundaries of community. There is, though – just contingently – a more far-reaching 'slope' of generalization. The fact is that beyond the many highly specific pains or troubles, joys and triumphs, known to people only in virtue of the specificities of their particular culture, there are also some highly general afflictions and misfortunes from which they can suffer merely in virtue of their human and animal traits, in virtue, that is, of their nature; as there are by the same token some very general conditions of well-being, protections and provisions that are the minima of any reasonably comfortable or fulfilled existence. That this is so allows and encourages people, everywhere, to say such things as: this should not be done to a *man* or a *woman*, and that is what is owed to a *human being*, and it is wrong to deal with a *person* thus and right to treat them so – allows and encourages them to say such things in addition to anything else that might be said about the treatment proper to more narrowly specified categories of other people. To repeat, there may be no logical necessity about any of this. It is not hard nevertheless to see why such a language and its kinds of reasons, pertaining to general human goods and especially ills – to pain, hunger, illness or disease, to mockery and insult, to assault upon the integrity, of the body, or the mind, or the beliefs – are rather more common, and more commonly taken for compelling in moral reflection and argument, than are utterances of the ilk: certain poets spoke as they did, or it just happened, or we just do.[40]

Now, of course, there are always complex mediations between this type of generalizing, tendentially universalist, discourse and the more specific rules and habits of conduct. There are applications, adjustments and exceptions. There are qualifying and countervailing considerations. And human beings seem to manage rather well to find their way to living with or actually bringing about the misery of other human beings. Still, they seem generally to need and to give themselves reasons for doing this when they do it, reasons which will override or obscure for them those other more general considerations. *These* people, they might say, are evil or they are our enemies; by the way they have behaved or in the way they live they have forfeited all compassion and respect; they are degenerate; and so on. The very need, however, for such countervailing reasons testifies in its way to the *prima facie* force of the universalizing ones, and there is a particular putative reason here above all which does this. It is the suggestion that some group of people is not really made up of human beings at all. It is the discourse of *dehumanization*.

Nothing shows more tellingly the power, and the widespread recognition of the power, of arguments from a common humanity than the extensive use through human history of linguistic and other practices of dehumanization. Doing other people serious harm, the perpetrators do not just say that it is because these others are evil or are enemies. They do not just say that it is because they are strangers or foreigners. In logic, they could do this, why not? They could say: we extend moral respect only to 'Members' (naming some given community) and then work altogether consistently from there. But that is not in general the way. They do not or do not only say: these people are not 'Members'; are not Germans or Aryans, or whites. They say or they imply, and they do things which make it easier for them to think: these are not human beings.

Rorty calls up the figure of the consistent, sophisticated Nazi. It is a common move whenever a stereotype is needed for the moral alien, someone adopting ethical premises supposedly quite distinct from our own. But it is not a bad idea here to give attention to the figures of actual Nazis, and of their accomplices. Agents of the most hideous evil of our century, even such people did not typically find sufficient to their purpose some set of different, wholly other, moral axioms, forthrightly upheld and consistently applied. On the contrary, they had recourse to every device of falsehood, denial, concealment and euphemism, of symbolic and spatial separation of their intended victims, of psychological and physical degradation of them, in order to hide from others and from themselves the enormity of what they were doing.

Rorty, as it happens, himself has some observations on this 'theme of dehumanization'. Commenting, in his Amnesty lecture, on a report of atrocities from Bosnia, he says:

The moral to be drawn . . . is that Serbian murderers and rapists do not think of themselves as violating human rights. For they are not doing these things to fellow human beings, but to *Muslims*. They are not being inhuman, but rather are discriminating between the true humans and the pseudohumans. They are making the same sort of distinction as the Crusaders made between humans and infidel dogs, and the Black Muslims make between humans and blue-eyed devils. The founder of my university was able both to own slaves and to think it self-evident that all men were endowed by their creator with certain inalienable rights. He had convinced himself that the consciousness of Blacks, like that of animals, 'participate[s] more of sensation than reflection.' Like the Serbs, Mr. Jefferson did not think of himself as violating *human* rights.[41]

Well, it is Rorty who says it. Out of his own mouth we have an answer to the claims that were our point of departure here. If the theme of dehumanization is as common as he rightly says it is, this shows that 'because she is a human being' is a less weak and more convincing moral consideration than he says *it* is. Recall, equally, his denial that the notion 'one of us' carries any great force construed as '"one of us human beings" (as opposed to animals, vegetables, machines)'.[42] The widespread tendency to dehumanize potential victims tells otherwise. It tells, what Rorty fails to recognize behind the merely different verbal form, that the notion '(fellow) human being' – as opposed to infidel dog and devil, to demonic force or poison, to parasite, to vermin – is, for human beings, an extremely powerful mode of moral inclusion.

As for the importance of sentiment, finally, about this we can be more brief. It is possible both to acknowledge it and to decline once more to be bound by the Rortian alternative on offer: sentiment *as against* rationality, argument, enquiry and the rest. Crucial as it obviously is, sentiment alone could not possibly be enough to a moral consciousness, liberal or other, wedded to the aim of wide solidarity; and the reason why it could not is quickly explicable in terms of Rorty's own favoured examples and genres. Reading or watching a sad and sentimental story intended to acquaint us with other, different kinds of people will not educate anyone who cannot see beyond *that* story: from Tom or Eliza to what it was to be a slave in the American South or is to be a slave anywhere; from *Schindler's List* to what it meant to be a Jew in Nazi Europe or means to be a person to whom anything at all may be done; from a report about Bosnia, or now Rwanda, to the seemingly never-ending extremity of what bystanders are willing quite passively to witness. You can close the book with a tear for these folk, leave the cinema feeling 'awful', turn away from the set appalled at what people in countries 'like that' are able to bring themselves to do.

Nothing follows if you come away with no more general or deeper understanding than how sad it was, no grasp of its possible relevance to you or to anything other than itself, no more intense moral or practical commitment. If, on the other hand, through comparative, generalizing, sensitive reflection – or by the faculty, put more simply, of thought – you do come away with something like this or even only have it reinforced, then you are, just so, already on the terrain of wider reasons and principles, of possible argument and counter-argument, of enquiry, theory, the works. Sentiment is all well and good, and indispensable. But the objects of it can be very particular. In any world where relations are not entirely face to face, *a fortiori* when the context is this, the present world, and a discussion about wide-ranging solidarity such as might reach people who are many and distant, the necessity of a generalizing moral rationality to work together with decent human sentiments would seem to be elementary.

III

I conclude this chapter with some comments specifically on Rorty's Amnesty lecture. A reaction to it I have met with is that it marks a significant shift by him, away from the anti-universalist views he had previously put forward.[43] This reaction is understandable in view of the lecture's subject – human rights, a somewhat universalist notion – and of the warmth Rorty expresses there for the human rights culture. Nevertheless, except in one thing, just the new-found warmth of expression, I do not for my own part read his lecture as embodying any fundamental change of view. Hitherto, reference by Rorty to human rights has invariably been negative and dismissive. Just as, he told us, we should not take our common humanity as a philosophical foundation for democratic politics, nor should we take 'natural human rights' for one either.[44] The conviction that 'the point of social organization is to let everybody have a chance at self-creation' was not to be 'based on a view about universally shared human ends, human rights, the nature of rationality, the Good for Man . . .'[45] Rorty wanted to take his distance from the kind of liberals who 'hold on to the Enlightenment notion that there is something called a common human nature, a metaphysical substrate in which things called "rights" are embedded . . .'[46]

Now, never mind that that is a prejudicial way of formulating the notion of rights. Contemporary sponsors of this notion are not obliged to think of human rights as 'things' or as embedded in a metaphysical substrate. We can think of them simply as moral claims: claims that individuals can make, and that can be made on their behalf, and which we take to be legitimate, all in virtue only of the humanity of the individuals – no metaphysical substrate, but the *physical* and *neurological* and *psychological* make-up of those individuals as human beings. We can think of human rights as the justified entitlements of all such beings. But never mind, because the point is that, even formulated so, the notion of human rights depends on others which in Rorty's eyes are no better than, if they are at all different from, a metaphysical substrate. So it makes a kind of sense (for him) to formulate the notion in a way which will be (for others) prejudicial. This is quite at home in a viewpoint in which we are regularly enjoined to stay away from the idea of human universals in general, and from the idea of a common humanity in particular such as one might appeal to in justification precisely of certain general moral claims called human rights. It all makes a kind of sense.

But then there comes a day, and Rorty gets up and endorses the thought that the human rights culture is a welcome fact of our world and morally superior to other cultures.[47] A change of heart? In something, obviously yes: it is the thumbs-up instead of the thumbs-down. In everything else, however, no. For the whole structure of ideas we have become familiar with from his earlier work remains intact. Thus, there is no human nature, there is only open possibility: the sole lesson of history and anthropology, Rorty tells his audience, is our malleability; we need not ask what we really are, for we can make ourselves into whatever we are clever and courageous enough to imagine ourselves becoming.[48] Respect for human dignity (enclosed by him in scare-quotes) does not presuppose any 'distinctively human attribute', nor the superiority of the human rights culture count in favour of the existence of 'a universal human nature'.[49] And there is nothing relevant to our moral choices in 'a purportedly ahistorical human nature'.[50] Rorty is happy with the inference that, in affirming the human rights culture without support of 'outmoded' foundations, one 'denies the existence of morally relevant transcultural facts'. Moral relevance, for him, resides still in the shared identity of a moral community.[51] And the road away, so to say, from the consequences of that – which can produce this: 'a rational agent in the only relevant sense[:] the sense in which rational agency is synonymous with membership in *our* moral community' – is still the road of 'expand[ing] the reference of the terms "our kind of people" and "people like us"'.[52]

Rorty *only* neglects to explain what need there could be of rights properly qualified as 'human' if there really were no morally relevant transcultural facts, no transcultural fact in particular of a common human nature. In these circumstances there would still be a place, certainly, for special rights: rights appropriate for this, and other rights appropriate for that, lot of people; rights fashioned to fit the characteristics – capacities, interests or needs – acquired in virtue of these forms of acculturation, different rights fashioned for those forms and for the quite other characteristics produced by them. But it would not seem apt, it would seem indeed perverse, to put such rights under the rubric of universal 'human' rights when it is their cultural specificity, tailored to historical and social differences, that marks them. As to wholly general rights, needed across these differences, the notion appears no longer to be meaningful in the absence of characteristics common across all differences and relevant to how one thinks people ought to be treated. One would not then be able to envisage the need even for such rights as the right against having one's body and mind broken by torture; or a right to minimal subsistence (as required for pursuing any project, culturally specific as may be); or the right to worship any God or none without being made to suffer merely for doing that. So the human rights culture looks to me like a misnomer for any moral outlook Rorty could, on the basis of his favourite themes and emphases, consistently support.

On the other hand, maybe it is not a misnomer, and one can continue – puzzlingly – to envisage the need for such general or universal human rights even in the absence of morally relevant transcultural facts. One could adduce in their favour then, though, only morally irrelevant facts, transcultural or otherwise (a right against torture because of the light shed by the moon or because I saw the phrase written on a wall); or morally relevant but culturally specific facts, such as that those rights are part of our tradition. In that case, one endorses the human rights culture just anyway as it were, willy-nilly. For if the facts adduced in its favour are morally irrelevant, that is what they are. And if the facts adduced are of the type only, 'these rights are part of our tradition', it is part of the same broad tradition to be able to offer some reasons in favour of what you support apart from that you support it – to offer some such reasons and not only reasons *against* what you support. His new-found warmth of expression for the human rights culture, therefore, does not in my view represent a significant shift on Rorty's part. It is a shift rather in the manner of the parable of the critic and the Elder, or of the parable of the Mentor and the wandering girl. It is a change, to put this otherwise, from rejecting the reasons of the moral outlook to commending the moral outlook whose reasons they are. But for what kind of reasons then, is as pertinent a question here as it was there.

And yet. And yet. This may not be altogether fair. For Rorty does offer some reasons. They turn out to be not unfamiliar ones. In fact, everything renounced by him is, here as elsewhere, in this lecture as in the rest of his work, retrieved. Pressing the virtues, for example, of the sentimental story as against the 'universalistic notion', he speaks of stories which begin so: 'Because this is what it is like to be in her situation – to be far from home, among strangers'. Or which begin so: 'Because her mother would grieve for her.' He speaks, too, of a progress of sentiments that consists in 'an increasing ability to see the similarities between ourselves and people very unlike us as outweighing the differences'.[53] But now, 'grief' and 'mother' and 'home', do they not just begin to edge one toward a possible terrain of morally relevant transcultural facts? And similarities with 'people very unlike us' that can nevertheless come, these similarities, to be seen as outweighing the differences, do they not point after all to *something* shared, the common traits of a humanly general make-up?

Rorty perhaps senses the discomfort of this type of question. For, just at the point where he comes upon the outweighing similarities, he hastens to add that it is 'not a matter of sharing a deep true self', only of 'such little, superficial, similarities as cherishing our parents and our children – similarities that do not interestingly distinguish us from many nonhuman animals'. A diversion, no more. I leave aside that cherishing one's loved ones can be as deep as deep gets; and that there are also, remember, pain and humiliation, not such little or superficial matters either. But Rorty here overlooks that elsewhere in this very lecture a human nature is denied by him not only in the sense of the distinctively human, but also in the sense of the transcultural, the universal, the ahistorical. And he here overlooks that elsewhere in the same lecture allusion is made by him as well to qualities that do interestingly distinguish us from other known animals, such as allow him to speak of us as the 'self-shaping' animal, and as 'exceptionally talented animals'; although this is set by him (to me a bit strangely) against our being the 'rational' animal. Moreover, we 'can feel *for each other*', he thinks it is useful to say, 'to a much greater extent than [other animals] can'.[54]

So it goes. And so much the better for Rorty that he does retrieve what he energetically, indefatigably, repudiates. So much the worse, however, for a solidarity and a liberalism without foundations.

Notes

Bibliographical details for the works of Rorty referred to here, and the abbreviations used for them, may be found at p. 147.

1. See Chapter 1.
2. CIS, pp. 191–2.
3. HRS, pp. 115–16.
4. CIS, p. 191. Emphases original.
5. CIS, pp. 190–91.
6. CIS, pp. 190, 198.
7. PMN, p. 382 n. 24.
8. PMN, pp. 190–92.
9. ORT, p. 200.
10. PMN, p. 192.
11. CIS, p. 192.
12. CIS, p. 196.
13. CIS, p. 198.
14. CIS, pp. 113 n. 13, 116; TWO, p. 151.
15. CIS, p. 190. And see pp. 9, 14 above.
16. Terry Eagleton has some fun with this, and to good effect, in 'Defending the Free World', *Socialist Register 1990*, p. 85.
17. See text to notes 11 and 12 above.
18. CoP, pp. 207–8; CIS, pp. 68, 84. And cf. EHO, p. 198.
19. ORT, pp. 201–2.
20. See ORT, pp. 176, 197.

21. CIS, p. 192.

22. CIS, pp. 60–61. And cf. pp. 93, 185.

23. Which is suggested to me, obliquely, by ORT, pp. 23, 38; and TWO, p. 149.

24. In a recent interview, Rorty makes some observations about secularism and democracy. He speaks as follows: 'The public sphere simply can't be served by people who say: "I'm not going to give you any argument for this but it's against my religion so I'm not about to tolerate it".' And as follows: '. . . to say it's against my religion isn't an argument. If you can give some reasons that don't have to do with revelation, then the question of whether or not your belief is held because of your religion is irrelevant. You can just produce the arguments. If you say "It's just against my religion, and that's as far as I can go", then you're stepping outside of your responsibilities as a citizen.' Which seems pertinent to the issue here. Or do 'traditions' enjoy a privilege that religions don't? See 'Towards a liberal Utopia: An interview with Richard Rorty', *Times Literary Supplement*, 24 June 1994, p. 14.

25. See ORT, p. 207.

26. TWO, pp. 148–9.

27. See text to note 18 above.

28. CIS, p. 192.

29. See text to notes 18 and 21 above.

30. Something like the question posed here is posed in other terms by Rorty himself at CIS, p. 88. If he provides a satisfactory answer to it in the pages following, this reader has been unable to find it. Cf. the text to note 40 of Chapter 2 above.

31. CIS, p. 173.

32. CIS, pp. xv, 197.

33. EHO, p. 198.

34. TWO, p. 141.

35. ORT, pp. 207–8.

36. PMN, pp. 190–91.

37. CIS, p. 16.

38. TrF, pp. 636–9. And cf. TWO, pp. 148–9.

39. HRS, pp. 118–19, 122, 125, 128.

40. References at notes 22 and 25 above.

41. HRS, p. 112.

42. See the quotations in the text to note 5 above.

43. I refer here to suggestions I have encountered in response to conference and seminar presentations of the arguments of this book.

44. CIS, p. 196.

45. CIS, p. 84.

46. ORT, p. 207.

47. HRS, pp. 115–16.
48. HRS, pp. 115, 121–2.
49. HRS, p. 116.
50. HRS, p. 119.
51. HRS, pp. 116–17.
52. HRS, pp. 123–4.
53. HRS, pp. 133, 129.
54. HRS, p. 122.

4

Language, Truth and Justice

I shall be travelling in what follows a somewhat winding road, and so here is my central thesis. If there is no truth, there is no injustice. Stated less simplistically, if truth is wholly relativized or internalized to particular discourses or language games or social practices, there is no injustice. The victims and protesters of any *putative* injustice are deprived of their last and often best weapon, that of telling what really happened. They can only tell their story, which is something else. Morally and politically, therefore, anything goes.

I begin with two snatches from Primo Levi, for they delineate the space in which I shall want to situate myself. In *Moments of Reprieve* Levi explains why he would not write too freely about a close friend while this friend was alive: finding oneself with another, even more favourable, image than one's own self-image can be painful. Reflecting on the plurality of possible images of a person Levi writes: 'What the "true" image of each of us may be is a meaningless question.' In *The Drowned and the Saved*, on the other hand, Levi recounts an episode in which a schoolboy lays out for him an escape plan which would have liberated him from Auschwitz had he but managed to think of it. In a trivial way the episode illustrates, Levi says, 'the gap that exists and grows wider every year between things as they were down there and things as they are represented by the current imagination . . .'[1]

Such is the space in which I place myself. There is not just one true image of a person or description of an event or state of affairs. Different angles of vision and personal beliefs, different political, cultural or other purposes, different linguistic and conceptual frameworks, will shape and colour the content of any description or narrative, yielding a plurality of possible representations of whatever is the subject at hand. Yet there is, for all that, a *way things were down there*, a reality constraining the range of adequate description, interpretation and explanation.

Now, thanks principally to post-modernist currents, there is abroad these days a regrettable intellectual influence, or so I view it anyway, a radical relativism that would block this last kind of judgement. I mean, as I shall throughout, a cognitive, and not a moral, relativism. That is what I shall be engaging with in the present chapter: with cognitive relativism, in the form it assumes in the writings of Richard Rorty. There is an initial difficulty with this, however. Like many relativists, Rorty is in the habit of denying that he is one. I shall follow Hilary Putnam in his brisk way with this apparent difficulty. As Putnam has put it:

> I shall count a philosopher as a cultural relativist for our purposes if I have not been able to find anyone who can explain to me why he *isn't* a cultural relativist. Thus I count Richard Rorty as a cultural relativist because his explicit formulations are relativist ones . . .[2]

I believe Putnam is right on this point, but more about that in due course.

Rorty's politics are not my politics. Still, there is a set of overlapping values here. It is a familiar theme: liberalism and socialism, the common heritage of the Enlightenment, the path or the paths, painful, disputed, obscure, towards a feasible utopia. Precisely that shared heritage of aims and problems prompts the question for me of whether justice – or freedom, democracy, minimizing needless suffering – could be served by cognitive-relativist viewpoints. Saying this should suffice to make clear, too, that my primary terrain will be neither philosophy of language nor philosophy of science, more suitable domains, it might be thought, for tackling the issue of truth. It will be rather political philosophy, broadly construed: as taking in, that is to say, the concerns also of history, social theory, ethics. As it is, I stick my neck out somewhat. But if more justification is needed for choosing the terrain I have chosen than that this is the one of most pressing interest to me, then here that justification is. Rorty (not to speak of others of similar mind) himself brings his relativizing discourse on to the same terrain. And there cannot be, in any case, an exclusive disciplinary domain or philosophical discourse on the question of truth. It is too important to be monopolized by anybody.

One last preliminary which I shall want as a reference point. There is a style of argument one can meet with, it seems, on any sort of topic. Some reasonably straightforward and uncontentious point will be so formulated as to appear extremely bold and startling. But it is bold and startling only by virtue of being put in a way that, taken seriously, makes it in fact absurd. When its extravagance is pointed out to the proponent of the argument, she or he will fall back on the more obvious and uncontentious, the less interesting, version of their thesis . . . but without quite giving up the extravagant one. And so on. My own main experience of the form is this. Marxists often used to say and some of them still do, as indeed do plenty of other kinds of social critic besides, that there is no human nature; everything is historically formed, socially determined, culturally specific, and the like. When you point out in response to them that there are certainly transhistorical human needs and capacities, you get the reply: 'Oh well, if *that's* what you mean by human nature . . . But we meant that people are not [for example] intrinsically cruel or selfish or possessive; and/or that the character of individuals is significantly shaped by the specificities of their society and culture.' It turns out, in other words, that there *is* a human nature, on the moment at least. Only it does not contain qualities which are not (or not thought by your interlocutors to be)

universal ones, and there are many such non-universal qualities – two propositions unlikely to surprise anyone.

Rorty, as I have documented in Chapter 2, is a partisan – or
a prisoner – of this particular thematic variant of the argu-
mentative style, a style, as I also mentioned there, that was
summed up nicely by J. L. Austin in the following words:
'There's the bit where you say it and the bit where you take it
back.'[3] A second thesis I shall be offering in what follows is
that a parallel exists between Rorty's positions on language,
truth and reality and his views about human nature. It is only
by taking back what he himself actively propounds that he
can escape the unhappy moral consequences of it which I
seek to indicate here in my central thesis already announced.

I

In this section I outline briefly Rorty's pragmatist, anti-realist
philosophical positions. One link to what has gone before in
Chapter 2 is this. Rorty, we saw there, affirming that socialization 'goes all the way down', would discourage us from
thinking of the human being as 'an ahistorical natural kind
with a permanent set of intrinsic features'. The effort so to discourage us is expressive of a wider 'anti-essentialist' ambition.
For according to him not only is human nature not a natural
kind, there are no natural kinds. There are no 'intrinsic
natures' of things, simply there as it were, primitively given.[4]
Just as, with us humans, socialization goes all the way down,
so also for things generally does *language* go all the way
down.[5] Or contexts do:

> The essentialist philosopher, the one who wants to hold on to the
> notion of 'intrinsic, context-independent, property' says that the
> 'it' which inquiry puts in context *has* to be something precon-
> textual. The antiessentialist rejoins by insisting that it is contexts
> all the way down.[6]

As Rorty also puts this point:

The intuitive realist . . . thinks that, deep down beneath all the
texts, there is something which is not just one more text but that
to which various texts are trying to be 'adequate.' The pragmatist
does not think that there is anything like that.[7]

We have to drop 'the notion of a God's eye point of view, a
way the world is apart from our descriptions of it in language'.[8] Notions, equally, like 'hard fact' and 'matters of fact'
are absurd, 'unfortunate relics of metaphysical thought'. The
idea of 'an objective public world which is not of our
making . . . [is] no more than out-dated rhetoric'.[9]

Is Rorty saying what he seems to be saying? That there is
not, then, a way things were or are down there, not 'a Way
The World Is', as he himself in one place puts this to warn all
sensible people off it?[10] Well, he does seem to be – when he
says it. The idea of 'something which is what it is apart from
language, apart from any description' is one of 'the pseudo-
problems created by the essentialist tradition'. 'A pragmatist
must . . . insist', Rorty says, 'that there is no such thing as the
way the thing is in itself, under no description, apart from any
use to which human beings might want to put it.'[11]

We have, accordingly, to jettison a whole group of
metaphors that is entrenched within our thinking about
knowledge and truth: metaphors of vision and mirroring; 'the
picture theory of language' and truth as accuracy of representation; what John Dewey called the 'spectator theory'.[12]
With those metaphors goes also the idea of some representations or vocabularies having a 'privileged' or more 'adequate'
relation to reality.[13] 'There is no description which is some-
how "closer" . . .' to what is being explained, there is only the
explanation which best suits a given purpose.[14] A Rortian
subtext here is that there survives in such representational
conceptions of knowledge a 'religious need to have [our]
human projects underwritten by a nonhuman authority'; there
is a notion in them of non-human forces to which we are
responsible.[15] We must be, instead, self-reliant, giving up that
notion in favour of solidarity with the community with which

we identify. '[W]hat matters is our loyalty to other human beings clinging together against the dark, not our hope of getting things right.'[16]

We should let go of any idea, consequently, of knowledge or truth as correspondence. This is 'an uncashable and out-worn metaphor' of which several hundred years of effort have failed to make useful sense.[17] 'How could we ever tell?' – how tell that our language fits the world? For 'you can't compare your beliefs with something that isn't a belief to see if they correspond.'[18] The reason why you can't has already been given one formula: there is no God's eye point of view. This reason is repeated by Rorty in different terms. There is no way to get outside our beliefs, or to step outside language, or to compare thought 'with bare, unmediated reality', 'reality plain, unmasked, naked to our gaze'.[19] Again, there is no 'skyhook' which could lift us clear of our beliefs in order to see the world thus plain.[20] '[T]he world does not provide us with any criterion of choice between alternative metaphors . . .', Rorty says; 'we can only compare languages or metaphors with one another, not with something beyond language called "fact".'[21]

By way of alternative to the metaphors of correspondence, he offers us other metaphors. Language is a tool or set of tools, and vocabularies are instruments, rather than pictures and representations – they are 'tools for dealing with the world for one or another purpose'.[22] We gauge them, there-fore, not by correspondence or fit, but by how far they enable us to cope: to cope with the pursuit of happiness, our needs, our wants.[23] We gauge them by how far they are useful to us, give us the power of persuasion.[24] Or we may think of knowledge also, not as confrontation (in the sense of interaction) with reality, but as conversation.[25] '[T]here are no constraints on enquiry save conversational ones – no wholesale constraints derived from the nature of the objects . . .'[26] This is to say that knowledge is to be treated as justified belief or warranted assertibility, one's community, whether social or scholarly, being the source of epistemic

112

authority.[27] 'Objectivity', in so far as it retains a meaning, becomes consensus.[28] And a key norm within this is coherence: coherence amongst our propositions and amongst our stories.[29]

As I shall be expressing some doubts about these positions, it may be as well to start by acknowledging the difficulty with correspondence as a would-be comprehensive explication of the notion of truth. With any medium- to large-scale theory about or way of explaining or interpreting a series of events or set of social relations or other sort of cultural or natural reality, we will not have altogether independent access to the two domains supposedly to be compared for correspondence.[30] It is not as if we can just really *look* at the global object-domain and then in turn at the explanation or interpretation or theory. To the extent that we gain access to the realities in question here through the languages and concepts in which we think, and that these are the medium also of our beliefs about and understandings of those realities, we do not have quite separate domains for comparison. Metaphors of correspondence cannot capture all the specificities, nor the complexity, of those human relations to the world which are belief, knowledge, understanding, and so on. The ensemble of what we sometimes call representations does not actually depict or map the realities of which they are representations in the same manner as pictures and maps.

Yet I do wonder, all the same, about some of the formulations from Rorty's work that have been rehearsed above. In the next section, I shall first articulate a few of my doubts about them, albeit rather tentatively. The questions and associated suggestions and arguments that I offer there are offered in a spirit precisely of doubt – and of a worry about ulterior normative consequences. Not entirely confident, however, as to the weight, either singly or in conjunction, of these critical questions, suggestions and arguments of mine, I proceed from them to a more immanent form of critique, putting in question the internal coherence of Rorty's views. I try to show thereby the substantial sense in which those views are relativist ones, before going on to consider some of the moral implications of their being so.

To anticipate the general drift of the next section, it is as follows. The claim that language goes all the way down is of a kind, indeed, with the claim that socialization goes all the way down. Because there is with us humans a culture, there is not (it is said) a human nature. So, equally, because we apprehend the world through language, there is not a way things are in themselves. And because we apprehend the world through language, there are not any matters of fact, and we can only compare beliefs, languages, metaphors, with each other, not with fact. But are these propositions actually any more sustainable than the denial, nearly always taken back, of a human nature? As this denial would have us move from the premiss of culture towards a kind of imperializing culturalism, so would those propositions urge us from the premiss of language to an inflation of the linguistic which all but obliterates or, better, swallows up the objects of language. It is as though we had no other choice but between such an inflation on the one hand, and a pure, passive-receptor, blank-sheet empiricism on the other, wherein language is no more than a neutral code by means of which the realities out there just uniformly imprint themselves.

We are forbidden, it appears, from thinking that, central as languages and vocabularies are to how we receive, how we shape, construct and present the understandings we come to, still we are constrained also by the realities we seek to grasp: constrained by facts which do verily intrude themselves, 'through' language, but not exclusively through language; constrained by things which *are* simply given to us, whether more directly as in perception, or less directly through various types of evidence – collected to be sure, but also 'thrown up' or 'left behind'. And we are forbidden then too, seemingly, from supposing that such constraints as these do give us some bases of choice between the various different discursive offerings in the field, even if they do not bind us to the certain selection of a single one.

But if there is not some middle way like this and we really cannot speak here, consequently, of more and less 'adequate' or of 'closer', we need to discover what *else* will enable us to avoid a relativism for which the choice between different views is pretty well only a matter of taste.

II

Here is a first question. It concerns whether language really does go all, rather than only much, of the way down. I have this cat, Mimi, affectionately known as Meems. I can tell her apart from other cats. I do not think this is by dint either of her names or of words like 'tabby', 'white', 'smallish' and so forth. For she, Meems, for her part has no difficulty in distinguishing me from a squirrel and from other human beings. Experiments by Piaget show that the human infant acquires, before it acquires language, an understanding of the permanence of objects: the awareness that an object may persist when not directly present to sense. Think how important these two kinds of knowledge are, the perceptual differentiation between different creatures or individuals, and an understanding that objects can continue to exist even though no longer 'there'. If cats and infants have such knowledge without language, why not also adult human beings, with it? Do we lose non-linguistic forms of awareness by acquiring language, so that this is not like adding one skill to another already acquired and now retained, but more like reaching the top of a ladder which is then pulled away? It would be interesting to hear an argument for the view that we do lose, with the acquisition of language, all other forms of awareness.

Think of sexual pleasure and of pain. Think of performative knowledge, like how to walk or how to ride a bicycle; or how to play a piece of music on the piano, no longer remembering or never having been able to read the written score. Think of knowing roughly where to look for the sound of a voice, and knowing – instantly – that it is a voice; or of seeing as you open your eyes that it is no longer dark; or of smelling

115

as you re-enter the house that something unusual has happened while you were out; or of knowing exactly where to put your hand in catching a ball. Think of hearing – instantly – that the sound just uttered was the sound of the word 'discourse' and not the words 'joy' or 'movie', nor any of an enormous number of other vocal sounds, both words and non-words, you would also hear immediately they were uttered.

We relate to the world in and through language, certainly. The point of these foregoing questions and promptings is neither to quarrel with that nor even to deny the extent to which language affects and transforms our other capacities. It is only to point out that as well as through language, through discursively structured and propositional belief, we relate to the world through a whole battery of other skills, perceptual and practical. We 'move within' these also; they are as indispensable as language to our modes of receiving and conceiving nearly any sort of reality. To speak as if language were the all-embracing, absolutely sovereign medium of cognition and awareness, always 'vocabularies', 'metaphors', 'beliefs' and such forming the prism (prison?) between us and any outer light; to say, as Rorty does discussing Heidegger, that 'there is no nonlinguistic access to Being'[31] – this seems at least one-sided. Might we not say just as well that there is no non-perceptual access to Being? Which, bearing in mind the consequences and products of abstraction, analysis and deep theory, would be equally one-sided and, not to beat about the bush, probably false.

A second question now, on the subject of metaphors. Yes, this is what picturing and representation are, they are only metaphors for knowledge or truth. As such they do have their limitations. But do they not also have their uses? I say, for example, knowing or believing it to be so, 'Richard Rorty is in the vicinity. Please find him; he looks like this.' I hold up my copy of *Contingency, Irony, and Solidarity*, bearing a photograph of Rorty on its front cover. What tool or implement would serve as effectively? Or consider how the jury's verdict in a courtroom might depend upon, or appear dubious in the light of, the video evidence of some relevant episode. Giving a description *can* be like showing a picture. 'The town hall is a white building fronted by columns, with a central clock tower; it looks out over a tree-lined square.' Or: 'They forced him to the ground and beat him repeatedly with their batons.' Having this sort of description, you are more like someone with an actual photograph or piece of film than you are like someone with an implement or with nothing at all. Then again, conversation and tool-using are also in the present context only metaphors. Whatever they may help to illuminate, they have limitations of their own. Exclusively by conversation in a sealed room, a group of people will never be able to discover what is going on in Bosnia. And persons, as Rorty himself insists, are separable from the tools, in a way that they are not separable from the languages, they use.[32]

So picturing (or mirroring, or vision) is not an adequate metaphor for all the characteristics and practices of knowledge. But that is because no *single* metaphor will do. Knowledge is *sui generis*. It does have, nevertheless, its representational and its observational moments, as well as its conversational and transformational ones. And metaphors of representation and correspondence, their limitations as metaphors notwithstanding, do at least preserve the sense of something independent out there beyond the representational process or artefact itself, and of knowledge or belief as different from but related to it, not wholly internalized or self-enclosed. They preserve the sense that, as Thomas Nagel has written, 'Language reaches beyond itself . . .'[33]

My third question, then, has to do with this 'beyond', and it can be approached by way of the conversational metaphor. Conversation, as it happens, secretes an element, its own constantly recurring moment, of confrontation (in the sense of interaction) with reality. For if the stuff of conversation is words, these must be exchanged back and forth by the use of hearing and vision or else of touch. To put it otherwise, you may 'get at' the world mostly through language, but it is equally the case that you can only 'get at' language through the world: via the shapes and the noises which we employ as words. Why not take *this* as your starting point, and then make language rather than the Way The World Is vanishingly small in relation to the other? If you could not know through confrontation with reality, then nor could you know, either, through conversation with your peers, since you would have no means of knowing what they had written or said. You would have no access to anybody's words. However much language and vocabularies and metaphors are the medium and compose the substance of knowledge or belief, they should not be allowed to get above themselves when it is the perception of shapes and sounds, that impressive practical ability instantly to recognize and tell these apart, which is the modest but ever-present companion of language itself. It puts on fewer airs. But it is the factotum, so to say, without which all language, as well as the best and worst of metaphors, would be lost.

Now, there is here what I believe to be a cogent argument against theses of the sort, 'no such thing as the way the thing is in itself' or as the 'way the world is apart from our descriptions of it in language'.[34] The argument in a nutshell is that conversation as between separate intelligences itself presupposes a structured and differentiated segment of public 'matter' between them, independently of their jointly finding or deciding or agreeing that it is so structured and differentiated. The point is that in order jointly to find, decide, agree or indeed disagree about anything, those intelligences, the persons communicating, need what I shall call tokens – shapes, noises, gestures – to be the bearers of their differentiated meanings. For instance, and paring things down rather for simplicity of exposition, they will need tokens of affirmation and negation. Any old couple would do: respectively, a nod and a shake of the head, a tree and a fish, * and @, 'ooh' and 'ah', 'yes' and 'no'. But the parties to the conversation would not be able jointly and consistently to identify or agree as being different, tokens which were not actually different. One cannot make sense of that idea: of *what* it is they would then be doing and of *how* they would be managing to do it.

The argument says, in other words, that differences between the shapes and sounds (or whatever) employed as meaning-tokens cannot be such only through perception or by convention. How would this work? The conversing parties jointly and systematically find sets of similarities and differences within, or else they agree to treat as such sets of similarities and differences . . . what? Undifferentiated sameness? An altogether fluid and unstable chaos? How do they pick out what to register or agree as being different from or similar to anything else, never mind how get the success rate they get in mutually consistent identifications? Notice that this argument does not trade on any assumption that the tokens are natural objects. They may in principle be any kind of thing: gestures, artefacts, conventional shapes, instrumental sounds. The point is only that, come into being as they may, they must form a field of objective similarities and differences if they are to be usable as a medium of communication.

Where one view, therefore, is that language's sovereignty over all access to the world means there cannot be a way things are just in themselves, the argument put here is that there *must be* a segment of the world which is already – in itself, and however we may then further construct or conceptualize that world – structured, somewhat stable and differentiated. Otherwise language across a public space with shared symbols would be impossible. But if there must be such a segment of reality, then there *can* be other such segments of it, simply there the way they are, irrespective of how or even whether we talk or think about them. There not only can be other such segments. Here, too, there must be – at least if my argument is good. For this argument can be generalized, beyond those specific differentiations involved in having separate meaning-tokens, to other kinds of differentiation beside. It cannot of course be extended to all other kinds of them, since there are some in which the differences are wholly linguistic-conventional: as is the difference between a Tuesday and a Friday, or between the owner and any non-owner of a piece of property; between the powers of a pawn and the powers of a rook; between the status of being the first and that of being the last letter in an alphabet; and between being the capital of a country and being some other place in it. It may be said even of differences like these, however, in which it is the convention that makes the whole difference, that in order to mark them as differences we need the different marks. So that in fact the trail of the world's serpent is on all human conversation.

Well, this is if the argument is good. And maybe it isn't good, nor any of its preceding sister arguments and questions either. In that case I hope there are better arguments, more telling or pertinent questions, to the same sort of end, because if not, the implications are worrying. Or so I shall now try to show by coming back to the issue of relativism. I want to explore the internal configuration of some of Rorty's ideas as they relate to this issue.

Rorty regularly disavows relativism. He does not, he asserts, hold every belief about a topic to be as good as every other. It is a viewpoint he knows to be self-refuting.[35] Nobody, indeed, could fairly or sensibly doubt that he does regard some beliefs as better than others. He so regards a secular outlook, for example, vis-à-vis a religious one.[36]. What is less clear is what he offers that would make any ranking of beliefs more than an arbitrary, unarguable preference. To forestall predictable 'misreadings' here, be it noted that this is not a quest on my part for an easy criterion or rule that will generate for us the One Right Answer or Only Truth. It is a search merely for indices and guidelines enabling us to make a case of some kind: always tentative and provisional, with its own problems and uncertainties despite anything that might be said in its favour, but nevertheless, as things currently stand, a case – in the way of reasons for thinking that this or that view is better than this or that other one, and for thinking, more importantly, that there are some views which are seriously worse.

It is a strange notion of relativism to propose that just having some ranking of viewpoints avoids it. If the ranking is no more than an unreasoned preference (as with a matter of taste such as a preference for cheese over marmalade), or if it can be grounded on considerations recognized only by those sharing the same preference, then there is no common terrain or set of standards on or by which to reason and compare as between the viewpoints being ranked. The preference itself becomes in effect its own reason. While that may leave you and me or anybody with the view(s) deemed better by each one, for any non-monolithic *us* there is merely the bunch of preferences. Without common means of judgement, public to the human intelligence, matters of truth and knowledge can then be assessed only relative to each private, or sectional, or culturally specific 'point of view'. That looks like a passable definition of the relativist predicament. I shall take up two types of relevant theme from Rorty's work: a) one in which he appears simply to concede his conviction of an absence of compelling general criteria for the ranking of viewpoints and beliefs; and b) another which may seem to offer us a route away from the thoroughgoing relativism this implies, but which turns out upon inspection not to do so.

a) Rorty himself insists that alternative 'final vocabularies' as he calls them, competing language games, opposed intellectual worlds, are incommensurable. There are no neutral criteria or grounds or reasons to be had for adjudicating between them. We lack ways of arguing in favour of one and against another that are non-circular. This incommensurability applies, for instance, in the case of Galileo and Cardinal Bellarmine on the disposition of the heavens or movement of the planets.[37] As is only logical Rorty then often forswears, or so he says, the use of argument in his own behalf. With regard to the philosophical viewpoints he puts on offer, he will not argue, he tells us; rather he will change the subject. What, on his own account of things, he also does is to try to make the vocabulary he prefers *look* better than the vocabulary of objection to it. Thus:

Conforming to my own precepts, I am not going to offer arguments against the vocabulary I want to replace. Instead I am going to try to make the vocabulary I favour look attractive by showing how it may be used to describe a variety of topics.

And:

So my strategy will be to try to make the vocabulary in which these objections are phrased look bad, thereby changing the subject . . .[38]

It should be noted, however, that Rorty thinks that 'anything can be made to look good or bad by being redescribed'. There is no real standard in the matter of better and worse descriptions: '. . . although the thoroughgoing ironist can use the notion of a "better description," he has no criterion for the application of this term.'[39] I come back to that last point shortly.

But it is a puzzling business, this trying to make 'look' good. I am not alone among Rorty's readers in finding that, his disclaimers notwithstanding, he does give every appearance of arguing for his positions, much as other writers do. Arguing is the way, precisely, in which he seeks to make an intellectual position look good – or bad. He does it generally by means that are very familiar: putting forward a consideration here, giving a countering reason there, claiming of an idea that it does not make sense, attempting to demonstrate that it does not, and so on. Why not otherwise – if it really is about looks and not about arguments – simply try to make the view you oppose look bad by presenting your audience with appropriately unflattering *pictures* of it? Who knows, but perhaps there is something like this involved in the suggestion that people of foundationalist inclination really yearn still for the comforts to be derived from belief in a divinity.[40] In any case, we may move on. In the style and spirit of Rorty's conversation that kind of thing does not (as with others of similar mind whom one might think of here it does) have an inordinate place. The significant point in the present context is that if we take him at his word on the subject of incommensurable vocabularies or language games, of anything being able to be made to look good or bad by means of a redescription, it would seem to follow that we lack non-arbitrary grounds for distinguishing between better views and worse ones.

b) I move on to themes which might be read as taking us away from out-and-out relativism. One of them is the theme of coping, or 'instrumental' success.[41] On occasion Rorty presents this notion in terms suggesting that *it* might give us a way of distinguishing cognitively better from cognitively worse; as when he says that 'modern science does not enable us to cope because it corresponds, it just plain enables us to cope'.[42] But the impression is misleading. Were anyone to conclude from this that it is, then, coping rather than correspondence with fact which is the standard for ranking theories or beliefs, they would be too hasty. For 'just plain' enabling us to cope is not a concept available to Rorty, as he must be aware. There are at least two reasons why it is not. First – and as he is aware – there is a plurality of different purposes against which to estimate whether or not any theory, belief or language game helps us to cope.[43] Second, even for some one given purpose, it would not be credible in view of the rest of what he thinks for him to offer coping in or toward that purpose as a logically basic, would-be objective datum. What counts as coping or working, as instrumental success, must be also for its part subject to interpretation, to belief-laden, language-governed understanding. We have it indeed from Rorty himself that anything can be made to look, not only good or bad, but also 'useful or useless', by being redescribed.[44]

Coping, therefore, does not take us away from, it leads us back into, the incommensurability of alternative vocabularies. Appearing to furnish by implication some neutral yardstick,[45] it actually poses as its own question: coping with, or in, what? Here Rorty may allow himself sometimes to say 'coping with the world'.[46] But coping and not coping with the world are themselves features of the world – of which it is asserted that there is not a Way It Is apart from our descriptions of it. With the powers imputed by him to description, anything must also be construable, presumably, as (useful) coping or as (useless) failure to cope.

These are not conclusions merely foisted on Rorty against his own intended meaning. They are inferences I think he would willingly embrace. It is altogether in their spirit that he should speak in one place, for example, of 'the laissez-faire attitude that sees religion and science as alternative ways of solving life's problems, to be distinguished by success or failure, rather than rationality or irrationality'. Approving this laissez-faire attitude, the attitude of the 'holistic pragmatist', he goes on to speak likewise of 'adopt[ing] naturalism without thinking of ourselves as more rational than our theistic friends'.[47] Commendable as the sentiment may be by way of commitment to a pluralist social ethic or principle of personal conduct or both, does it not cast in another light Rorty's effort to present the philosophical realist, the foundationalist, in the guise of someone with a 'religious need' – for comfort and metaphysical reassurance? If coping is the name of the game and if it helps some people, in coping, to look for and find such comfort, then the game is over, surely. Why use the beliefs of these people in invidious comparisons? You know, seekers after divinity and all that. Unless there is another covert, and covertly realist, set of rules, according to which one may continue to play on the idea that it is weak and self-deluding to take comfort from . . . what isn't *really* there.

Or, putting aside this comparison now and treating the beliefs of the philosophical realist in their own right, as separable from a belief in gods, one might consider whether the coping theme does not render Rorty's anti-foundationalist position self-refuting (in another way than the one he anticipates and tries to counter by rejecting the relativist label). I do believe a pretty good case can be made, anyway, for the view that it enables most people to cope better with the world if they permit themselves to think that there *are* some ways it is apart from their, or our, descriptions of it. The people whom this kind of thought enables to cope better include Richard Rorty himself, a matter to which I return in the next section. A second theme we might consider as possibly providing a route away from cognitive relativism, is that of coherence. If accurate representation is for Rorty a vain image of the point of intellectual enquiry, the ambition of overall coherence better characterizes it. One should, or one can, he holds, try 'to make one's web of belief as coherent, and as perspicuously structured, as possible'. He sees himself, indeed, as one of those philosophers 'who think of rationality as simply the attempt at such coherence'.[48] To the extent that he would want to give it this kind of honoured place in his thinking, however, the exigency of coherence just seems to be *there* in Rorty, as it were primitively, like some original 'essence' of sound thought. To be sure, one important way amongst others of discriminating better from worse in intellectual matters is to attend to the degree of mutual consistency of the theses, propositions or beliefs in any given ensemble of them. All the same, his readers might care to ponder why such a norm should matter to someone holding Rorty's other views.

In John Fowles's novel, *The French Lieutenant's Woman*, we are offered two different endings which are, speaking pedantically, mutually incompatible. In my own experience, readers of the book do not on this account describe it as incoherent. In a historical or social-scientific work, on the other hand, they might well so describe a similar sort of thing. Why should they do that? Could we not simply agree, within the community of scholarship in question, to transfer these other 'looser', or these different, these literary, norms to the study of social and historical realities; henceforth allowing that the same particular event might both have occurred and not occurred, that more general explanatory hypotheses might be entertained simultaneously presupposing the occurrence and non-occurrence of the one event or presence and absence of a given person at an identical place, and so forth?

That it cannot – if it cannot – simply be agreed to proceed

in this freer spirit would seem to suggest that we do labour here under a constraint: an external or an internal constraint, but in any case more than merely facultative or acceptable with our community. It could be that there is something about the nature of the realities forming the object of historical and social-scientific enquiry, or it could be that there is something about the way we, human beings, apprehend them, something that cannot accommodate the kind of simultaneity or conjunction we call a 'contradiction'. No matter. Either way or both, the coherentist philosopher has upon his hands what he had hoped to be rid of, constraining 'rational' conversation, culturally specific as it may be. He has a nature of the realities, or a nature of logical thought; and, from this last, some general features of the human mind, and perhaps therefore something of a human nature. He has, *horribile dictu*, foundations. Or, then again, maybe he does not. Maybe we *could* just agree – without loss, without sacrificing the means towards better and against worse views – to transfer the freest, the most anarchic, norms to the study of history and society.

Rorty owes us, in sum, an explanation for any putatively general exigency of coherence. Otherwise coherence itself can only ever be at most a name for the internal rules, the localized forms, of a given vocabulary or language game. It, too, would be unable to settle anything as between language games. Could it be because he senses or even thoroughly appreciates this that Rorty is, in another voice, apparently not so taken with coherence after all? Coherence for him, it sometimes seems, is a matter only of presentation. The distinction between the rational and the non-rational, upheld and defended at need, can also be made light of when the time is right. So:

> The ironist thinks that such arguments – logical arguments – are all very well in their way, and useful as expository devices, but in the end not much more than ways of getting people to change their practices without admitting they have done so.

Again:

> Nor is there ['in the ironist view'] much occasion to use the distinctions between logic and rhetoric . . . or between rational and nonrational methods of changing other people's minds.[49]

This is (as one might say) coherent with the advertised Rortian self-denial in respect of the use of argument.

We have reached a convenient juncture at which to raise a question some might think long overdue in a book about Richard Rorty. The question is this. Is there any point in engaging critically with the work of a writer subscribing to opinions like the ones just quoted? Does it make sense to argue with the views of the self-proclaimed ironist who forswears the use of argument himself? Could it matter, inside the language games of ironists and pragmatists or of 'post'-ists, all this exploration of the relations, whether of implication or self-contradiction, between the ironist's various positions, this sustained interest in precisely their internal coherence, more generally this contention with them, now over one issue and now over another?

I am not entirely sure of the answer, frankly. For on the one hand, and taking the question first *ad personam*, Rorty himself does keep coming back with declarations about, seemingly, the value of coherence. It is a persistent emphasis of his, a repeated commitment.[50] In line with it, he has lately confessed himself hurt by the imputation to him of a certain frivolity: that he will 'say anything to get a gasp'.[51] On the other hand, he does regularly give out signals of an opposite kind as well, signals tending to demote logical argument, or argument, period. And the suggestion which he reports as being hurtful to him is itself testimony that there are other of his readers than this one who find that he can be rather cavalier.

Perhaps I will just leave it here that, in so far as Rorty cares to present his moral and political ideas as coherent, and in so far as he does do, willy-nilly, what many people would call arguing for them, I care to engage with those ideas on the same basis; trying to show, by argument, where I think they are not coherent or are questionable in some other way. And in so far as Rorty and others who share his attitude do not care for any of this, that is, of course, their right. There is a gesture I cherish, which I remember my friend David Sanders going through from time to time: a gradual, a prolonged, extending of the arms, with simultaneous shrugging of the shoulders and appropriate facial expression, displaying . . . what exactly? . . . a put-upon fortitude, and lingering, resigned perplexity; and saying, approximately (or this is how I always construed it), 'So, *what* can you do?' The description, though, doesn't really give you the thing fully. You would need to *see* it. Anyway, in so far as there are those who do not care for argument and the like – that.

And, whether they care for argument or not, one may still try to suggest to anyone interested, why making light of rational methods of discourse, why making all truth and coherence relative to competing language games, is not the best way of defending humane democratic values.

III

I now do what is seldom done in this sort of matter, so far as I am aware. Moving forward under the simple assumption that Rorty means what he says, I take the anti-realist pronouncements at face value.

If there is no truth, there is no injustice. If truth is wholly relativized or internalized to a language game, final vocabulary, framework of instrumental success, culturally specific set of beliefs or practice of justification, there is no injustice.

Let me begin here. An insistent, recurring, feature in the testimony of victims of great injustice is: bear witness. One Ali Bourequat comes out of a Moroccan jail after nineteen years without charge or trial, having suffered severe tortures. I have only one passion, he says, truth.[52] Another, Jacob Celemenski, Holocaust survivor, writes, 'Today I am one of the survivors.

For twenty years I have constantly heard within my mind the very cry of the murdered: Tell it to the world!'[53] This is the cry of the Holocaust dead, and it is the burden also of those who have managed to survive them. It is: 'remember and tell, remember and tell.'[54] It is the reported last words of the historian Simon Dubnow: *'shreibt un farshreibt'* (write and record).[55] It is: 'You must get out of here alive, you must bear witness to our suffering.' It is: 'to dream and pray for the day to come when I could go free and tell the world, "This is what I saw with my own eyes . . ."' It is: 'to show the world what I had seen and lived through, on behalf of the millions who had seen it also – but could no longer speak'.[56]

Primo Levi, the century's best known and perhaps also wisest witness of this, its most infamous enormity, has given us some reflections on the figure of the witness. In a chapter entitled 'The Memory of the Offence', he discusses the intricate nature of memory, its now shifting or fading, its now misleadingly fixed, forms. He searches to capture the subtleties and the difficulty of remembering well, and the ease as well as self-serving deceptions – as amongst the generality of perpetrators – in remembering badly. It begins, the remembering badly, with the very crime perpetrated, clouded as it was in secrecy and euphemism, 'the entire history of the brief "millenial Reich" . . . a war against memory, an Orwellian falsification of memory, falsification of reality . . .'[57] And then, also, Levi relates in *If This Is A Man* a dream which tormented many of the prisoners at Auschwitz: a dream of being at home once more and of the intense pleasure of this, of recounting what had befallen them – and of being met with indifference and disbelief on the part of friends and loved ones. In the dream itself a 'desolating grief', and on waking a live residue of anguish, follow, Levi remembers, upon this response. 'Why does it happen? Why is the pain of every day translated so constantly into our dreams, in the ever-repeated scene of the unlistened-to story?'[58]

'Constantly to remind', the Spanish writer Jorge Semprun, who was imprisoned at Buchenwald, says in a recent interview.

'We have to repeat endlessly so that successive generations do not forget . . . Historical memory is crucial because the experience of evil is not transferable.'[59] The experience of evil. It is a matter not only of the past but also of the present. In a report earlier this year about East Timor, John Pilger recalls Levi's dream of the unlistened-to story: 'This "radical gap" between victim and listener, as psychiatrists call it, may well be suffered en masse by the East Timorese . . . "Who knows about our country?" they ask constantly. "Who can imagine what has happened to us?" '[60]

I think one may set aside the suggestion that only some lingering religiosity could account for the feeling of a need and responsibility to be faithful to something 'out there', beyond the intellectual or conversational process: a 'things as they were down there' in Levi's own earlier-quoted phrase,[61] or a things as they are today somewhere else, the pre-given subjects indeed *of* belief or knowledge, of memory, of historical enquiry. Divinity does not come into it. Solidarity with other people is a sufficient motive. For 'human beings clinging together against the dark' is right.[62] Unfortunately, all too often the dark comes not from the brute cosmos, but from other human beings. A beginning in such cases, morally and politically, is the illumination of knowing what has happened, of knowing 'the truth' about it as people will sometimes over-simplifyingly say.

Let it be clear here: I do not want to be misunderstood to be using the example of the Holocaust (therefore misusing it) to belabour someone for views he does not hold. I do not mean that Richard Rorty might overlook, belittle or deny the enormity of this experience and its constituent horrors. From the various references to it in his work it is clear that he does not. I simply ask, in the conversational spirit he himself sponsors, how Rorty's positions as earlier outlined would enable him, and us, to discriminate better, more compelling, accounts of or claims about this particular segment of history from less compelling and worse ones. I ask if it is possible for him to do that without free-riding upon views he has seen fit to reject.

And, to repeat the point, I discount in asking this his frequent implication that foundationalists and their like must all hanker after one single correct account of things or version of the truth: after 'the One Right Representation', 'The One Right Description', 'the necessity that inquiry should someday converge to a single point', 'the true story about how things are', and so on.[63] No. There will, there must, be many stories about this, as about any other, historical catastrophe or merely event, many which are viable although differing from one another. There is bound to be such a multiplicity of attempts, interesting and informative, persuasive or at least arguable, to understand and explain or just report on some smaller or larger aspect of it. This is a banality, surely, not worth too much of anyone's energy – in view of the diversity of individual perspectives on the 'one' historical experience, of the immensity, in every sense, of what happened across a continent, of the unevenness and the gaps in the extant documentation, of the sensitivities and the pain which the subject arouses. It is by now a well-rehearsed theme of Holocaust research and discussion that there cannot be here any single, much less any obvious, way of writing or trying to 'represent' or understand; nor even a way of communicating fully what the victims went through, from those who directly suffered it to people who did not.

So a plurality then, certainly, of voices and stories, of efforts to grasp and to convey something. Yet, when all this has been duly registered and emphasized, a set of questions still remains. How if at all are we able to speak of stories or accounts that are weaker, less good, not to be given credence on some point? How speak about claims and putative descriptions which are *wrong*? Can we do this without recourse to a 'way things were down there'? What resources, if any, does Rorty give us?

I now generalize the issue. Rorty will sometimes urge upon his readers the idea that his 'ironist' outlook is well-suited to a democratic and liberal society.[64] I have already offered in earlier chapters some reasons for doubting this, and on the

131

matter under discussion I believe we have another one. For consider the place of justice in any such polity. One does not have to agree with Rorty's claim that 'contemporary democratic societies are *already* organized around the need for continual exposure of suffering and injustice';[65] one may find it exaggerated and a bit complacent, if it is not merely hasty and ill-considered. But a democratic polity worth the name must, in any event, deploy some more or less effective means of redressing, and of trying to remove or at least diminish, various different kinds of injustice. And this is a special problem for the ironist, because to do that presupposes an ability to get at what is, oversimplifyingly, called 'the truth'. Note that the point here is not that it would follow from Rorty's views that we could have many conceptions of justice, difficult to decide between. There *are* many and it *is* difficult. The point is the rather more elementary one that, whatever the conception, to operate principles of justice, you need to know what has happened or is the case, under some passable interpretation of it within the multiplicity of these that there must, of course, always be.

Take, for example, what we call a miscarriage of justice. What *is* that? How could it matter as much as we think it does if it were only the simultaneous availability of alternative stories? But on the basis of Rorty's preferred notions there could always be a good story to show how someone had done something which, as a naive old foundationalist might put it, they hadn't *really* done. It is all too easy to envisage how the story that they had could be good, nevertheless, in terms of its enabling some people to cope in their chosen purpose, or of its being consensual amongst them; of its being coherent by the rules of some given language game or in the light of a belief which, indeed, rendered it coherent; or of its being simply 'attractive' on one or another conception of what is attractive. Exactly the same goes for stories from those, often governments, denying that they have done something dreadful to people, whose own experience and story if they are still able to tell one, or whose story as told by others, is that they have in fact done it (the deniers, that is, what they deny). There are language games, language rules, within or by which the 'facts' in the story denied are not recognized or constituted as being 'facts'. The notion of a language *game* is actually rather to the point here, since the objectives and rules of games can be as varied as you want and are not bound to respect anything outside themselves.

In either sort of case – the so-called miscarriage of justice or the alleged atrocity denied – the would-be victims of the injustice only have their story, and there is another story in town. How could this matter? How could it matter if there were no 'way things really are (or were)' in the given case? But Rorty cannot fall back, remember, on any 'way things really are (or were)' in order to favour, or to 'privilege', one story over another.

So much for justice. I shall not waste any time showing how the line of thought can be extended. Democracy? Well, were the elections free and fair or were they rigged? Freedom? Rorty is a proponent of free and open debate. He is now given to suggesting, even, that we should be 'content to call "true" whatever the upshot of such encounters [free and open ones] turns out to be'.[66] So. If we all silence her in what *we* all agree was a free and open encounter, *was* it a free and open encounter? How should we go about determining that? Are there no facts of the matter in the matter of how free she was to speak? And if there are not, does the availability of divergent stories about it matter? Is this not just healthily pluralistic, chiming in with a spirit of irony and play?

Enough. By now there will almost certainly be readers who feel I am up to no good. I must be doing something wrong. It cannot be what Rorty really thinks, surely, these inferences and constructions of mine. Here, I could just take the option of responding that, if it comes to that, how could there be a what-Rorty-really-thinks, since there is for him no 'really'? But I decline this option. I do not, for my own part, find it a useful way of speaking.

Maybe it isn't what he really thinks. For he avails himself

often enough of ordinary (and dare one say it, realist) 'fact' and 'truth' talk. Here are a few points. Rorty appears to allow significant weight to 'the principle that a notorious liar's reports do not count as evidence'. He makes reference to – as part of the 'relatively simple and obvious side of morality' which 'swings free of . . . metaphysics' – the precept that 'instructs us to tell the truth'. He implies in passing that there might be a legitimate question about the 'accuracy' of a commentator's description vis-à-vis the intentions of the author commented upon (Derrida, as it happens). He says that the conviction that 'the standard "bourgeois freedoms"' are a necessary prerequisite for giving everybody a chance at self-creation is based, not on any universalist belief, but 'on nothing more profound than the historical facts . . .'[67] And he says that:

> a lot of [social and economic] repression is so blatant and obvious that it does not take any great analytic skills or any great philosophical self-consciousness to see what is going on . . . to notice that millions of children in American ghettos grew up without hope while the U.S. government was preoccupied with making the rich richer – with assuring a greedy and selfish middle class that it was the salt of the earth.[68]

In similar vein, he invokes 'facts about economic oppression or class struggle' – like 'the impossibility of feeding countries like Haiti and Chad except by massive charity which the rich nations are too selfish to provide', and 'the unbreakable grip of the rich or the military on the governments of most of the Third World' – facts which the 'vocabulary of social democratic politics' in some sort suffices to describe, apparently, without need of 'theoretical reflection' or 'further sophistication by philosophers'.[69] In the explanation of 'well-known fact[s]' like these, 'we need no fancier theoretical notions than "greed", "selfishness", and "racial prejudice"', or just 'details about the activities of, for example, the United Fruit Company and Anaconda Copper in Washington's corridors of power'.[70]

They are facts which belong together with what Rorty calls the 'unphilosophical, straightforwardly empirical, question' of whether soviet imperialism was a threat.[71]

I remind readers that with Galileo and the Church, the issue of the movement of the planets, there we had incommensurable vocabularies. But with these kinds of issue, the understanding of words and actions, social practices and structures – with the likes of 'What was it you were a witness to?' or 'What was his part in it?'; with 'What did Derrida intend?'; with what are the preconditions of general self-creation, and what the symptoms and the causes of economic and social oppression, and what the determinants and the proofs of imperialist interference or of great power menace – here we have simple matters of truth and lies, and we have facts which are obvious, indeed blatant (the social world now standing up and positively *clamouring* to be known as what it is). Here we have 'straightforwardly' empirical questions.

So what is this all about? I shall offer two suggestions, exploring one of them only briefly, the other at greater length. The first is that this kind of 'fact' talk is precisely inverted comma talk, a species of everyday shorthand. Rorty has recourse to a familiar way of speaking but, any appearance to the contrary notwithstanding, he means to say only that these are obvious facts from within a given vocabulary or language game in which they are constituted as facts. He uses the terminology of obvious fact for convenience, presuming to address perhaps, or at least leaning toward, a certain kind of interlocutor. But he does not forget in doing this that the terminology of matters of fact is an 'unfortunate relic of metaphysical thought', and that there is *not* any way things just blatantly are, apart from all description. Nor does he forget that anything can be made to look good by being redescribed, and that the competing outlooks and vocabularies in which description and redescription go on are incommensurable. He speaks, in short, a familiar language, one of 'So it just obviously is'; but he does so taking the whole ironist-pragmatist position as read and put now in parenthesis, its work of giving this familiar language another, less familiar sense already done.

In that case we may move on and I shall do so. For Rorty would then really mean what I have taken him to mean, it is his talk rather of obvious facts which is misleading, and all the important questions remain. There would be no injustice; there would be only stories of injustice and other stories. But we have no common ground or criteria by which to rank these different stories. All we have is the multiplicity of human purposes and of ways of describing them, a sort of double superabundance in terms of which to decide what is coherent, what is useful and what is coping. But what is a *lie* in such a universe? Come on, if it enables anyone to cope. (I take it there is no need here to deal with the consideration that it might enable this only at the cost of covering up or perpetrating a hurt to someone else. 'Covering up' is a what-really-happened kind of notion, bound under anti-foundationalist assumptions to be transmuted into something like: telling a different story from the other one. 'Perpetrating', likewise, is such a story amongst other stories. Come on, if it enables anyone to cope.)

My second suggestion cuts the other way. It is that, contrary to what I have been assuming in this section with regard to his anti-realist pronouncements, Rorty does *not* always mean what he says – just in so far as he also takes back what he says. One way and another, this second suggestion is, he takes the anti-realist stuff back. Thus, a Way The World Is, renounced by him in the most emphatic terms, simply reappears under other names: among them causation. Causation, he tells us following Donald Davidson, 'is not under a description'. It seems, after all, that 'there are objects which are *causally* independent of human beliefs and desires', or whose 'causal powers' are; and that through epochal historical changes of language and belief 'the same causal forces' persist. Now, it is true that Rorty is careful in saying this to explain that 'facts', on the other hand, falling within the scope of language games and their rules, are something else than these 'unmediated causal forces', 'this nonlinguistic brutality'.[72] Fine. He is perfectly free to have it so. Out there, then, and unmediated, not facts, but causation, objects, causal forces. Out there, nevertheless, there is again, restored to us, something sounding mighty like the thing overtly denied: an extra-linguistic, extra-discursive domain or (in what he elsewhere refers to as being 'no more than outdated rhetoric') 'an objective public world . . . not of our making'. There is once more, as we were told also there was not, 'something precontextual'; 'something which is what it is apart from language, apart from any description'.[73] In a messy compromise between one of the terms Rorty uses and the one he refuses for it, there is what I shall henceforth call a *brute facticity*; albeit its name, by him, not the Way The World Is, but rather Causation and Causal Powers and Causal Forces.

This affirmation by Rorty of such a brute facticity forms part of a more general trope: the rejection of idealism. One might have thought that if there is not – as on the face of it in the anti-realist formulations there is not – a way things are or the world is apart from any description, this would have to mean that differently conceived or described worlds *are* different worlds. It is not so, however. Rorty disparages the view that, for example, Aristotle and Galileo lived in different worlds;[74] he 'wholeheartedly assents' to the thesis that 'most of the world is as it is whatever we think about it'; he is not in sympathy with any 'notion of nature as malleable to thought'.[75] No, 'the world is out there . . . it is not our creation . . . most things in space and time are the effects of causes which do not include human mental states.'[76]

But how could Rorty know any of this? In terms of all we have seen him to be so insistent about, how can he, coherently, even say it, when according to him we have no way of comparing the world *as it is* with what we *think* about the world? If we cannot compare our beliefs with something which is not a belief, if we can only compare languages and metaphors with one another, not with anything beyond language, if in the view of philosophers whom Rorty commends for it one should 'refuse to contrast the world with what the world is known as',[77] how can he, coherently, purport to speak about how the world is – whether the same or different, malleable or not, our creation or the effect of causes having nothing to do with our mental states – just and precisely 'whatever we think about it', which is to say irrespective of or apart from all the various and changing human conceptions of it?

I think the answer to this question is the one I anticipated in the last section. Like most people, Rorty needs some terms for the brute facticity of things, and if he cannot have this coherently, then incoherently it must be. For without it he cannot cope. He cannot cope with the overwhelming wave of paradox and absurdity which will follow upon losing the world, losing it, so to say, 'behind' one's beliefs about or languages describing . . . the world. He cannot cope with explaining how, if there is not something which is what it is apart from any description, there could then be something which pre-existed all description; as to the best of our knowledge there is. Rorty himself names what it is he wants to avoid. He says it is absurd 'that we make objects by using words'.[78] He takes his distance from the 'people nowadays who owlishly inform us "philosophy has *proved*" that language does not refer to anything nonlinguistic, and thus that everything one can talk about is a text'. Such claims, he says, 'falsely infer from "We can't think without concepts, or talk without words" to "We can't think or talk except about what has been created by our thought or talk".'[79] It is not clear to me, however, that there is a difference that makes any difference between the absurdity and false inference identified by him here and the sort of formulas he himself goes in for, to the effect that one cannot compare a belief with a non-belief, or that one can only compare languages and metaphors with one another.

Knowledge of what has come to be called the Holocaust did not originate out of a comparison only between beliefs. It arose from simple observation: by the victims themselves, of the things they actually saw, heard, felt, smelled – killings and brutalities 'beyond belief', gas chambers, corpses, chimneys; by bystander witnesses who also saw some part of what was done to the victims; in due course by soldiers with the liberating armies, journalists, cameramen, politicians. But what was seen and heard, what was witnessed, was not a belief about, not a name for, not a description or an interpretation or a concept of, a mass killing process and its products. It was the thing itself, your actual referent. It was the killing, the violence, the dead, the places and the means and the remains of it. Even at a further remove from any such object of possible enquiry, at the historian's desk, or in the courtroom, directly seeing (hearing and so on) plays its crucial part together with any comparison between beliefs. It does so via the weight given to mutually corroborative or convergent eyewitness testimonies and to other products of first-hand observation, as contained for instance in contemporary records and documents.

Anything known by people on the basis of what they have themselves observed is always known, to be sure, under some description and in the terms of a given vocabulary and set of concepts. It is not known, all the same, through a comparison of beliefs, languages or metaphors merely with one another. For if it is said that even what is seen and heard must be mediated through language and belief, and *therefore* we only ever have before us for comparison languages or beliefs, this is exactly on a par with saying that because we must talk in words, we can only talk about words. It is fallacious reasoning, though remarkably common. Since there is within some given unity or ensemble, so we will often be told, not only this sort of thing, but also that sort of thing, therefore there is only that sort of thing. Since there are, *amongst us human beings*, differentiating cultures, it follows that there is no human nature (or, in a more extreme variant, no nature *tout court*). Since access *to the world* is mediated through language and belief, we have access only to language and belief. Indeed? In that case, since access to the world is mediated *through* language and belief, we have access just to what is out there beyond them – as through an ether transparent as can be – and language and belief are themselves as nothing. The world is obvious.

But actually not. We do the best we can, trying to put together out of what we have the most coherent story or stories we can, always in a given vocabulary and in terms of some preferred concepts; but also differentiating, within what we have, as to the variable quality of it, the better and the worse, the more and the less certain. Under the rule or guiding ambition of coherence, amongst the elements to be put into coherent relationship are precisely the facts we know, as established with the best probability we can achieve, and as established by observing reality – what is out there, the brute facticity of it. For in the world or worlds, also, created and wrecked by human beings, there is a brute facticity: in the sense of causes, objects, structures, events, and even of meanings and intentions, which can be what they are 'whatever' a particular enquirer, group of enquirers, or even generational cohort of intellectuals, may think about them. If my cat is asleep on the bed, or if a certain group of men did not plant the bombs they are in jail for supposedly having planted, or if the Nazis brought about the deaths of millions of Jews, there is some core 'way things are' about this, every bit as much as there is one about certain natural causalities stretching from Aristotle's day to Galileo's and beyond. It constrains adequate belief.

In any case, when all has been said, and when all to be taken back has been taken back, where according to Rorty do things stand on this point? Some meanings are pretty clearly what they are and others are rather more elusive. That there is no human nature may appear to mean that there are no commonly shared traits amongst human beings; or it may appear to mean that there are none which are distinctively human; or it may appear to mean that there are none which are of universal moral import. Sustainable in the end is something rather more modest: like that all people do not aspire, and nor should they, to one very narrowly specified kind of goal, activity or character. That there is not a Way The World Is can sit beside, or reduce to, that there *is* one, only lower case: 'nonlinguistic brutality'. So, what finally of incommensurability, of the lack of common criteria of epistemological judgement, the absence of all extra-linguistic, extra-conversational constraints upon it?[80] Is *this*, perhaps, just what it is, as stated? Or is it, yet once more, something to be 'scaled down' – giving us, say, that in our reception and presentation of things, vocabularies are of some considerable importance? It is not easy to know.

I explain why it is not easy and conclude. There are passages in Rorty's writings in which it seems that a distinction *might* be acceptable to him along the following lines: a kind of brute facticity exists so long as we remain at the level of details; but when it comes to overall vocabularies or language games or theories, encompassing a multitude of details, the relationships between them, constitutive assumptions, meanings and procedures, here we are stuck with incommensurability. Incommensurability then, as one might put it, does not go all the way down. With particular beliefs, small, local matters within a framing outlook of interpretation or explanation, talk of there being correspondences with bits of the world may make some loose sense, and brute objects cause us to adopt or be justified in holding those beliefs. On the other hand, with whole outlooks or vocabularies themselves, no such external comparison and constraint apply.[81] It is tempting to grasp at the possibility this may seem to offer of moderating Rorty's incommensurability claims from their apparent radicalism and consequent relativism to something more manageably compatible with a notion of publicly accessible fact and therefore truth. There are, however, two problems about doing that.

The first is a problem of Rorty exegesis. The very distinction just sketched on the basis of what some passages in his work seem to suggest is also, in other passages, opposed by him. In the context of his 'pragmatist holism', Rorty finds dubious the distinctions between theory and evidence, between questions of language and questions of fact, between human 'takings' and an objective given. He proposes we might now erase 'the picture which Davidson calls "the dualism of scheme and content"'.[82] In that case, incommensurability, the lack of neutral standards or criteria as between different theories, languages and schemes, reaches, indeed, right the way down, right into all their respective details, and we have a stand-off of moderate and radical 'incommensurabilisms', vying for attention within the same canon. Perhaps this stand-off, however, and with it the exegetical problem, does not matter all that much. I offer the hypothesis in the light of the second problem.

For this is how things would now appear to stand. Either – (1) – incommensurability goes all the way down and even the so-called 'facts' in dispute between competing vocabularies or language games cannot be adjudicated except by the competing standards of each one. Or – (2) – incommensurability goes only some of the way down: so that there are no neutral standards by which to judge the vocabularies or language games themselves; but at a lower level as it were, with the brute facts, these ride free of the effects of incommensurability. However, (2) here simply succumbs to a paradox of self-reference. In the account it must give of itself, it could not possibly have the status of a lower-level, brute fact. That things break down in just this rather two-tone way (up there and about so far, incommensurable, down here in the lower reaches, simply brute), that none of the hardness at the bottom should extend, for its part, all the way *up* and give you something against which to lean while you contemplate the higher theories – this would have to have, when fully articulated and explained, the form of a quite complex and sophisticated conceptualization of the universe it purports to be about. Within (2) in other words, (2) itself, along with (1), is of that kind, namely, opposed vocabularies or language games, to which incommensurability is held to apply. Which means that, according to (2), there *are* brute facts in matters of detail; but, according to (2) simultaneously also, the view

142

that there are brute facts has no greater intellectual authority than the view that there are not, since it cannot be rationally adjudicated against it. It can be, only, preferred, the way you prefer one flavour of ice cream to another.

An alternative line of thought is that vocabularies and languages games are commensurable. I hope so. Because it doesn't make a whole lot of difference precisely how the world is lost, whether quickly as in (1), or just a bit more slowly as in (2). Either way, if the facts are wholly internalized to the language game, the implications are not good. If there is no truth, there is no injustice. Morally and politically anything goes. There are appalling language games always in preparation somewhere, now as much as ever. They will be 'played' by those looking for the chance of it in deadly earnest. It remains to be shown that, amongst our defences against them, we have anything better than the concepts of a common humanity, of universal rights, and of reasoning together to try to discover how things are, in order to minimize avoidable suffering and injustice.

Notes

Bibliographical details for the works of Rorty referred to here, and the abbreviations used for them, may be found at p. 147.

1. Primo Levi, *Moments of Reprieve*, London 1986, pp. 149–50; and Primo Levi, *The Drowned and the Saved*, London 1989, pp. 127–8.

2. Hilary Putnam, 'Why Reason Can't Be Naturalized', in Kenneth Baynes, ed., *After Philosophy: End or Transformation?*, Cambridge, Mass. 1987, p. 228.

3. J. L. Austin, *Sense and Sensibilia*, Oxford 1962, p. 2.

4. See Chapter 2, subsection I (a), and notes 4–8.

5. CoP, pp. xxix–xxx.

6. ORT, pp. 99–100.

7. CoP, p. xxxvii.

8. TrF, p. 633.

9. CoP, pp. 136–7; ORT pp. 148–9.

10. WAR, p. 42.

11. ORT, p. 99; EHO, p. 4.

12. PMN, p. 371; CoP, p. 67 (and ORT, p. 155); CoP, p. 16.

13. PMN, pp. 182, 361; CoP, p. xx.
14. ORT, p. 60.
15. CIS, pp. 52, 45.
16. ORT, pp. 17, 39; CoP, p. 166.
17. PMN, pp. 371-2; ORT, p. 79; CoP, pp. xvii, xxvi.
18. ORT, pp. 139, 83.
19. PMN, p. 178; CIS, p. 75; CoP, pp. xix, 139, 154.
20. ORT, pp. 9, 38.
21. CIS, p. 20.
22. CoP, p. xix; ORT, p. 118; EHO, pp. 3, 152; CIS, p. 21.
23. PMN, pp. 10-11, 269; CoP, pp. xliii, 16, 82, 86, 150-53, 162-3, 193, 198; ORT, p. 1; TrF, p. 641.
24. CoP, p. 195; CIS, pp. 4, 8-9; EHO, pp. 5, 125.
25. PMN, pp. 156-7, 163, 170-71.
26. CoP, p. 165.
27. PMN, pp. 9, 188; CoP, pp. xxv, xxxviii.
28. PMN, pp. 335, 337; ORT, p. 38.
29. PMN, pp. 159, 178-9; CoP, pp. xxv, 205; ORT, pp. 82, 96-7, 101, 106; EHO, pp. 30, 130; TrF, p. 640.
30. Cf. on this Hilary Putnam, *Reason, Truth and History*, Cambridge 1981, pp. 72-4.
31. EHO, p. 37.
32. CoP, p. xix.
33. Thomas Nagel, *The View from Nowhere*, Oxford 1986, p. 108.
34. See text to notes 8 and 11 above.
35. CoP, pp. 166-7; ORT, pp. 23-4, 202.
36. CoP, p. xxxviii; ORT p. 202.
37. PMN, pp. 328-33, 364; CoP, pp. xlii, 191; CIS, pp. 5, 9, 48, 73, 80; EHO, p. 121.
38. CIS, pp. 9, 44; CoP, p. xiv.
39. CIS, pp. 73, 99; and see also pp. 9, 113.
40. See, for example, CIS, p. 45.
41. See ORT, p. 193.
42. CoP, p. xvii.
43. See CIS, pp. 115-16; ORT, p. 60; EHO, pp. 127, 132-3; Fem p. 4; WAR, p. 41.
44. CIS, p. 7.
45. See Putnam, *Reason, Truth and History*, pp. 117-18; Roy Bhaskar, *Philosophy and the Idea of Freedom*, Oxford 1991, p. 16; and Bernard Williams, 'Auto-da-Fe: Consequences of Pragmatism', in Alan Malachowski, ed., *Reading Rorty*, Oxford 1990, p. 30.
46. ORT, p. 120.
47. ORT, p. 66.

48. HRS, p. 117. And cf. ORT, p. 106; EHO, p. 30.

49. CIS, pp. 78, 83.

50. See the references given at note 29 above.

51. TWO, p. 141.

52. *AIBS Journal* (Amnesty International British Section), June/July 1992, p. 11.

53. Jacob Glatstein et al., *Anthology of Holocaust Literature*, New York 1968, pp. 81–2.

54. Julien Hirshaut, *Jewish Martyrs of Pawiak*, New York 1982, p. 33.

55. See Michael R. Marrus, *The Holocaust in History*, London 1989, p. xiii; and Martin Gilbert, *The Holocaust: The Jewish Tragedy*, London 1987, pp. 229–30.

56. In turn: Claude Lanzmann, *Shoah: An Oral History of the Holocaust*, New York 1985, p. 165; Olga Lengyel, *Five Chimneys*, London 1989, p. 88; Eugene Heimler, *Night of the Mist*, London 1961, p. 128. On the general theme, see also Terrence Des Pres, *The Survivor*, New York 1976, pp. 27–50, and Elie Wiesel, *One Generation After*, London 1971, pp. 38–40.

57. *The Drowned and the Saved*, pp. 11–21; quoted matter at p. 18.

58. Primo Levi, *If This Is a Man, and The Truce*, London 1987, p. 66. And cf. *The Drowned and the Saved*, pp. 1–2.

59. Julie Flint, 'Against Oblivion', the *Guardian*, 23 September 1993.

60. John Pilger, 'The West's Dirty Wink', the *Guardian Weekend*, 12 February 1994, p. 11.

61. See text to note 1 above.

62. See text to note 16 above.

63. CoP, p. 133; CIS, p. 40 (and EHO, p. 77); ORT, p. 38; EHO, p. 152.

64. CIS, pp. 45, 197; ORT, p. 193.

65. EHO, p. 25 (emphasis in the original).

66. CIS, p. 52 – and cf. pp. 67, 68, 84; and ORT, pp. 42, 88.

67. In turn: CoP, p. xlvii n. 51; EHO, p. 153; CIS, pp. 124 and 84.

68. EHO, p. 135.

69. EHO, pp. 25–6.

70. TrF, p. 642.

71. Ths, p. 578 n. 25.

72. ORT, pp. 81, 101, 84, 160.

73. See text to notes 6, 9 and 11 above.

74. ORT, p. 48; and cf. PMN, p. 324.

75. CoP, p. xxvi; PMN 279. And cf. ORT, p. 5.

76. CIS, p. 5.

77. ORT, p. 12; and cf. text to notes 18 and 21 above.

78. PMN, p. 276.

79. CoP, pp. 154–5.

80. See text to note 21 above; and CIS, p. 80.

81. CoP, pp. xxix, 162–5; CIS, pp. 5, 6; ORT, pp. 79–80, 83, 106; EHO, p. 38.

82. ORT, pp. 40–41, 65, 129. And cf. Jane Heal, 'Pragmatism and Choosing to Believe', in Malachowski, ed., *Reading Rorty*, p. 104; and Putnam, *Reason, Truth and History*, pp. 118–19.

Note on Abbreviations

In the notes to each chapter, the following works of Richard Rorty are referred to in the abbreviated forms here given.

CIS   *Contingency, Irony, and Solidarity*, Cambridge 1989.
CoP   *Consequences of Pragmatism*, Hemel Hempstead 1982.
EHO   *Essays on Heidegger and others*, Cambridge 1991.
Fem   'Feminism and Pragmatism', *Radical Philosophy* 59, Autumn 1991, pp. 3-14.
HRS   'Human Rights, Rationality, and Sentimentality', in Stephen Shute and Susan Hurley, eds., *On Human Rights: The Oxford Amnesty Lectures 1993*, New York 1993, pp. 111–34.
ORT   *Objectivity, Relativism, and Truth*, Cambridge 1991.
PMN   *Philosophy and the Mirror of Nature*, Oxford 1980.
Ths   'Thugs and Theorists', *Political Theory* 15, 1987, pp. 564–80.
TrF   'Truth and Freedom: A Reply to Thomas McCarthy', *Critical Enquiry* 16, Spring 1990, pp. 633–43.
TWO   'Trotsky and the Wild Orchids', *Common Knowledge*, Winter 1992, pp. 140–53.
WAR   'We Anti-Representationalists', *Radical Philosophy* 60, Spring 1992, pp. 40–42.

Index

The name of Richard Rorty is omitted from this index.

Printed in the United States
by Baker & Taylor Publisher Services